BEYOND CIVICS

Beyond Civics

The Education
Democracy Needs

SANDRA EVERY DEAN, *Ed.D.*

PHILADELPHIA

2023

*To the talented and dedicated faculty and staff of
The Philadelphia School, 1983–2006,
who created an intellectual environment
where children and adults found
personal fulfillment, social well-being,
and joy in their daily life.*

There can be no keener revelation of a nation's soul than the way in which it treats its children.

Nelson Mandela

Contents

Introduction   3

1   My Journey: Toward a More Perfect Education   7

2   A Place Where It Works   14

3   Finding the Right People   31

4   Connecting with Faculty   36

5   Faculty Connecting with Each Other   46

6   Connecting with Students   53

7   In Their Own Words   69

8   Building Student Connections   74

9   Connecting with Families   81

10   The City: Beyond the School Walls   94

11   Connecting with the Natural World: Awe and Responsibility   97

12   All-School Theme: A Community of Learners   102

13   Unit Themes: Teaching Skills Through Integrated Disciplines   124

14   The Central Role of the Arts   131

15   A Conceptual Approach   142

16   Teacher Autonomy   146

17   Education of Character   153

18   Democracy Is Central   167

Contents

19 Multiculturalism and Addressing Racism 172

20 Professional Development: Connecting
to the Future 183

21 Outcomes 201

22 Closing Thoughts 215

Acknowledgments 221

BEYOND CIVICS

Introduction

Democracy has to be born anew every generation,
and education is its midwife.

John Dewey

DURING THE PAST several years, Americans have become ever more aware of vulnerabilities inherent in American democracy. The COVID pandemic, climate change, and the January 6th insurrection revealed long-festering crises at the core of our society. The murder of George Floyd by police made clear that promises of the Civil Rights Movement of the 1960s remain to be fulfilled. Disturbing popular and political responses to existential threats to our constitutional democracy sadly include authoritarian proclivities; denial of the need for social justice and equity; the roll-back of hard-fought legal victories regarding voting, reproductive, and LGBTQ+ rights; and the politicization of science-based mitigation of COVID and climate change.

As an educator for more than 60 years, I sadly attribute these threats to failures in educational policy and practice. However, I am not referring to the glaring, long-standing inequities of school funding that have resulted in dilapidated facilities, inadequate

Note: Throughout this book I will be referring to philosopher and educator John Dewey. The primary sources that have informed my understanding of Dewey are *Democracy and Education* (1916), *Moral Principles in Education* (1909), and *Experience and Education* (1938).

technology, and understaffing that have indisputably negatively impacted the education of children in communities of color. The divisive threats to our democracy are not coming from the people who have long endured these inequities. I locate the fault in too many of our nation's better-funded, majority-white elementary and high schools, deemed by their communities (and standardized test scores perhaps) as good schools. These schools have curricula, textbooks, and classroom practices that do not ask students to think critically, empathetically, or creatively. They lack racial, ethnic, and gender diversity among students, teachers, and administrators. Their teachers do not have sufficient opportunities for meaningful professional development. And, finally, most schools do not prioritize teaching the discerning skills necessary to participate as well-informed and responsible citizens in a democracy.

I have spent a good amount of time during these pandemic years reflecting on the philosophy and practices that characterized The Philadelphia School during my 23 years as school leader (1983–2006). The goals and practices of our independent elementary school were grounded in philosopher and educator John Dewey's progressive educational theory, now more than a century-old but often viewed today as new-fangled by its critics. Dewey envisioned schools as microcosms of the larger democratic society. Students and teachers were to learn from each other through interaction on respectful, equal terms. For Dewey, democracy depended on a citizenry well practiced in such interactions as working together, listening to the ideas and opinions of others, making compromises, and working toward solutions that benefit the common weal. At The Philadelphia School we helped children make sense of the complex, interconnected world around them, have an awareness of multiple perspectives, and tolerate and work through confusion. And we sought to teach by example. This is what civics should look like.

This book takes a look at the fundamental aspects of our school's "great experiment," an educational program thoughtfully crafted and refined by an extraordinary faculty dedicated to their vocation and devoted to their students. As an independent school, we were free to create our own curricula and tailor our program to meet the needs and interests of the children whose education was entrusted to us. This freedom was critical to our success. Yet I believe all schools, regardless of funding inequities, could implement much of our practice and philosophy to educate children for life in a democratic society. With equitable funding, more costly practices, particularly those that require increased staffing, would be possible. That is, as long as state legislators, school boards, and school leaders have the will and the vision to make them happen.

As I write, state legislators and local school boards across our nation are focusing their efforts on policies that ban books, curtail the teaching of Black and LGBTQ+ history and social justice, and reject science. They are pitting parents against educators and usurping and undermining the professionalism of American teachers. Imagine how Virginia's history and social studies teachers felt when state delegates mandated the teaching of a "Lincoln-Douglass" debate—mistaking Black social reformer Frederick Douglass for Senator Stephen Douglas.[1]

Some elected officials even advance the idea that some children are destined for careers that do not require them to meet educational proficiency standards, and therefore such standards are not necessary. In my home state of Pennsylvania, attorney John Krill, representing Senate President Pro Tempore Jake Corman in a landmark school funding case, asked why the state's academic standards mattered for students entering certain lines of work.

---

1. In January 2022, Wren Williams, a Republican and new member of the Virginia House of Delegates, proposed a new standard for regulating high school social studies curricula. It included a requirement that students learn about "the first debate between Abraham Lincoln and Frederick Douglass." This was a clear misunderstanding of the 1858 "Lincoln-Douglas debates," in which Stephen Douglas, a senator from Illinois, faced off against Abraham Lincoln on the issue of slavery.

What use would a carpenter have for biology? ...
Lest we forget, the Commonwealth has many, many
needs. ... I think there is a need for retail workers, people who know how to flip pizza crust. My point is, do
these proficiency standards actually in any way imag-
inable serve the needs of the Commonwealth such as
they should be mandatory across the board? I think the
answer is no.[2]

My sincere hope is that this book will remind educators
that we can counter today's dispiriting trends and support students—and each other—as we grapple to sustain our nation's
Great Experiment. By practicing, modeling, and imparting fundamental democratic values in the schoolhouse, they can construct a future that is more equitable, more compassionate, and
more just for all Americans. The aim of education is not only to
prepare children for entering the workforce. Education should
inspire children to lead a fuller and happier life. In her 2022
inaugural speech as president of the University of Pennsylvania,
Liz Magill said, "Many people no longer believe that knowledge,
education, service to others, arts and culture, are the surest path
to well-lived and better-lived lives. We require leaders broadly
and deeply learned, service minded, and bearing all of the hall-
marks of an excellent education."[3]

2. William Penn School District, et al. v. Pennsylvania Department of
Education, et al. The lawsuit went to trial in Commonwealth Court beginning November 12, 2021.
3. *The Pennsylvania Gazette*, Nov/Dec 2022, p. 28.

CHAPTER 1

My Journey

Toward a More Perfect Education

Philosophy begins in wonder.

Aristotle

ONE OF MY earliest and happiest childhood memories was the discovery of dusty attendance and grade books that my mother had used during her brief teaching career while supporting my father in medical school. I used these materials to play school. I taught my dolls, neighbors, friends, relatives, anyone who had the misfortune to be captured by me in my playroom. Even then, I recognized that my methods were not terribly effective, especially with my dolls.

As is the experience of many children, my career direction was influenced by parents. My mother dissuaded me from being a teacher; summing up her own experience, she explained that "teachers are not supported, not paid well, and not respected." Hence, I graduated from the Wharton School of the University of Pennsylvania with a degree in economics.

One year working as a corporate statistician thankfully did not quash an interest in the humanities or, ultimately, my childhood desire to be a teacher. From 1964 up until 1983, when I became principal of The Philadelphia School, my teaching career took a variety of twists and turns, each one prompting me to seek the most effective and dynamic means to teach and learn. Prior to receiving any training in education, I was hired in 1964 as a part-time mathematics teacher for sixth and ninth graders at Akiba Academy, an independent school in the Philadelphia suburbs. Although I loved teaching and my students, I recognized that I was not much of a teacher. I did not have the tools for creating the kind of excitement that I wanted for my students.

Thus began several years of graduate study at night after teaching all day and raising four young children. In lieu of student teaching while pursing my M.Ed. at Temple University, in 1970, I became a long-term substitute at the suburban Cynwyd Elementary School, where I managed to create a second-grade classroom experience that was as joyful and lively as I had hoped but more chaotic and fragmented than I wanted. It was at about this time that as a parent of four children—two in preschool and two in elementary school—I noticed a striking difference between the excitement and joy of discovery in the preschool classroom and the rather humdrum experience my older children were having in kindergarten and second grade, where basal readers and workbooks with rote math facts seemed to dim children's natural energy and curiosity for learning. There had to be a better way.

Beyond my own teaching and my graduate work at Temple University, three experiences had an out-sized, clarifying influence on my philosophy of education: studying with the brilliant art educator Violette de Mazia; taking part in a four-week workshop on interdisciplinary, thematic curriculum design with charismatic British educator Sybil Marshall; and attending a professional development class about the work of innovative curriculum theorist Hilda Taba.

DE MAZIA AND ART

I had been able to enroll in only one course in art history when I was a Wharton undergraduate, so in 1961—with a one-year-old at home and another child on the way—I somehow managed to embark on a three-year study of the philosophy of art at The Barnes Foundation,[1] then located in Lower Merion Township. It was at the Barnes that I had the great fortune to study under Violette de Mazia, who had been a colleague of founder Dr. Albert C. Barnes.

From the outset, teaching and learning at The Barnes Foundation were greatly informed by the work of American philosopher and educator John Dewey, a friend of Barnes, who took to heart Dewey's warning that "[t]oo much philosophy and too little natural reaction to experience, and a too limited experience, is exactly what is the matter with aesthetics. . . ."[2] Little did I know at the time that John Dewey, whose name had not come up during my Wharton studies, would have an enormous influence in my career as an educator.

De Mazia made me aware of the importance of experience as a foundation for learning. It is critical to create a bridge between a learner's experience and the content that the teacher wants the student to understand. Experience, in the Dewey sense, means taking the event you are in, assimilating it into previous knowledge, and forming a new construct. At the Barnes, we attended lectures, but only after we had roamed through the galleries for hours beforehand to study and observe. The lectures were held in the main gallery on the first floor, with the specific artwork being discussed taken off the wall and displayed at de Mazia's side. The more I learned in de Mazia's classes about light, line, color, design, and the traditions of painting, the more I saw in

1. The Barnes Foundation, now situated in Center City Philadelphia, was established by Dr. Albert C. Barnes in 1922 to promote the advancement of education and the appreciation of art. Barnes assembled one of the finest collections of European and American post-impressionist and early modernist works. It also includes African sculpture; Native American ceramics, jewelry, and textiles; and American decorative arts.

2. Quoted in a letter from Barnes to Dewey, 1930.10.16.

the galleries. The more I saw in the galleries, the better I understood and internalized de Mazia's lectures.

MARSHALL AND THEMATIC TEACHING

Another turning point in the evolution of my educational philosophy was a four-week study of thematic teaching with renowned English educator Sybil Marshall[3] in the summer of 1973. Each morning, I "left" Philadelphia and stepped into medieval England upon my arrival at the workshop held at a local Quaker school. I was one of a hundred or so participants, and each of us was assigned membership in one of the three principal social classes of medieval England: aristocracy, who fought for the kingdom; clergy, who prayed for all; and peasantry, who worked for all. Hence, the title of the theme was "The Three Alls: Fight for All, Pray for All, Work for All." I was a female peasant, which suited me just fine, having spent part of my childhood growing up in North Philadelphia's Brewerytown.

Each social class group researched medieval English history from the point of view of their assigned class; culminating group activities included painting a mural and writing and performing a play complete with scenery and costumes. A typical day was devoted to study of two or three of the following: history, needlepoint, recorder playing, chorus, medieval music, and literature. Marshall also gave lectures on the pedagogy involved in our lessons. We each had to complete a needlepoint design, keep a journal consistent with our particular role, compose and perform a ballad, and, of course, participate in all group activities. We had access to many primary and secondary sources to read and study, artifacts (including knight's armor, costumes),

---

3. Sybil Marshall's *Experiment in Education* (1963; reissued 1998) shared her teaching methods based on integrating subjects and encouraging children's creativity. Marshall brought knowledge to life. The current educational term for this method is "place-based learning."

recordings of Gregorian chants, and prints of paintings from the Middle Ages.

Immersion in all things medieval was so complete that participants often forgot to change into their street clothes to go home. Some of the costumed men put up with a good bit of heckling when they continued to work on their needlepoint on the train or bus in costume. At home I worked for several hours each night reading primary and secondary sources to understand the power structure of medieval England, the rights and responsibilities of each class of people, and the day-to-day lives of individuals. The study was so rich that it became clear that the study of just one aspect, such as the rise of the merchant class, for the entire month would not exhaust the subject. The more I studied, the more questions I had. More questions inspired more study.

Experiencing the power of authentic interdisciplinary study was not my only reward during Marshall's four-week workshop. Marshall taught me about the power of high expectations when coupled with a personal relationship between student and teacher. When I was having difficulty writing in my journal and creating a ballad, Marshall met with me and guided me through my struggles. She honestly and constructively criticized my first drafts, but when she read the final products and praised specific parts, I felt proud and gratified and eager to do more.

TABA AND CURRICULUM DEVELOPMENT

The third strong influence on my approach to teaching and learning was the work of curriculum theorist Hilda Taba, who believed that developing student thinking skills based on evidence is essential in a participatory democracy. Like Dewey, she argued that education for democracy was a critical component of schooling and that it needed to be experiential, where children learn to ask questions and to solve problems and resolve conflicts together. Further, she maintained that students can only develop these skills and make generalizations after data are organized. During my time teaching at the Merion School, I attended a professional development workshop on Taba's inductive teaching strategies. The workshop acquainted me with her Spiral of Curriculum Development, a graphic organizer designed to illustrate concept development. It provided strategies to help students develop thinking skills by gathering data, forming concepts, interpreting the data, and making generalizations based on the data.

These three discrete learning experiences impacted my career as a teacher and educational leader. All three occurred during a time when I was raising small children, working as a teacher, and earning a master's degree in education and a principal's certificate. Equally critical were the seven years (1971–1979) I spent teaching in an experimental classroom at the Merion School. It was there that I was able to put into practice much of what I had learned from Violette de Mazia at the Barnes and from Sybil Marshall's workshop. As mentioned earlier, it was at the Merion School that I was introduced to the work of Hilda Taba. And it was there where I learned the power of team teaching, vertical grouping,[4] and interdisciplinary teaching and learning.

My co-teacher and I were able to tailor our practice based on what was best for the children in our vertically grouped classroom. Nearly 25 years later, in 2006, one of my former students at Merion, reached out to me, writing, "Just wanted to say thank you and that, many years later, I still have very fond and vivid memories of our projects on ancient Greece, and more importantly, of being in a place where I had a teacher who made me feel like learning was a wonderful game that I was lucky enough to be invited to play."

Our work to teach skills as the need for them arose allowed for successful hands-on, problem-solving activities, such as rede-

---

4. Vertical grouping is when a group of mixed-aged pupils (for example, students who might otherwise be placed in separate first and second grade classrooms) are taught together. A fuller discussion of the practice appears in the next chapter.

signing the school's playground to better utilize the space and resolve actual student conflicts about use of the basketball court and play equipment. Solving this involved collecting data about use and time, measurements of the area, equipment, and understanding the budget available to make changes.[5]

Our "experiment" in Lower Merion unfortunately came to an end. Despite our presentations to the school administration about the effectiveness of our approach to teaching and learning, we were unsuccessful in persuading the school to continue with our interdisciplinary, team-taught program, and the school returned to the district-wide curriculum. I was disappointed that this well-resourced and well-respected public school district (the same district in which I had been educated through high school) was not flexible or visionary enough to implement the kind of program I was passionate about, even though students had made expected progress in reading and mathematics. I moved on to teach briefly in a vertically grouped fourth and fifth grade classroom at Germantown Friends School, and in 1982, I was ready to take on a leadership role and implement my educational philosophy and practices that had evolved over the course of my years as a teacher.

5. Through a grant received by the school from the National Science Foundation, I was able to design, implement, and manage a program called Unified Science and Mathematics for the Elementary School. Students looked for problems in the community and worked cooperatively to solve them often using power tools to create models for their solutions.

CHAPTER 2

A Place Where It Works

*The joy in learning is as indispensable in study
as breathing is in running.*

Simone Weil

In 1982, I was hired as the curriculum director of The Philadelphia School (TPS), a small, nonsectarian, independent K–8
school founded in 1972 by a group of Center City parents who
created an educational program based on the work of John
Dewey and British educators in the Infant School movement.[1]
The school nimbly responded to innovations in teaching and
learning. Its program was designed to use the city's rich cultural,
historical, and educational resources as extensions of the classroom. At the same time, the school was committed to teaching
young people to become responsible caretakers of the natural
environment, and it provided students with a "country" site that
they visited weekly. City Country Classroom—those were the
three Cs that became our mantra over the years.

I was thrilled that The Philadelphia School's philosophy was
consistent with my own. Teaching and learning at TPS were joyful, but the joy derived from authentic work—in-depth study of
content, the development of strong academic and critical thinking skills, and comfort in finding one's voice. Content was stud-

---

1. I was delighted to learn that the founding principal and a founding
teacher had attended a Sybil Marshall workshop in summer 1972.

ied deeply rather than broadly (i.e., "covering many topics"). The school recognized and respected children's natural tendency to engage with the world and to make meaning by connecting past experience with the new, thereby enlarging and enriching that experience. This was Dewey's educational philosophy in practice. I was excited to join this community of learners. In 1983, I became the head of school (I asked to be called "principal").

By now, the reader may have become aware that I have used the term "progressive" sparingly thus far in this book. Dewey had described his educational philosophy as progressive. But over the years "progressive" education has looked and evolved differently in different school settings. And that is fine, in most cases; thoughtful innovation should be prized in all schools. However, it seems to me that many progressive schools spend an inordinate amount of time defining the term "progressive" to their constituents. And for some reason, despite the fact that progressive educational philosophy dates back to the 19th century, it still seems to be perceived popularly as "new-fangled." In my practice and in my role as an educational leader, I came back again and again to Dewey's belief that educators "looking for a new movement in education should think about the deep and larger issues of education rather than in terms of the divisive 'ism' about education, even such an 'ism' as 'progressivism.'"[2]

I will now briefly touch upon the guiding principles and practices of the educational program of The Philadelphia School during my tenure as school leader. (In subsequent chapters, many will be discussed in greater detail.) Together they made our school a joyful, authentic community of learners, bringing to life Dewey's vision of an education that provided students with the experiences necessary to sustain democracy. Dewey believed that democracy was possible only if an informed and participatory citizenry was comfortable interacting with one another and questioning and revising beliefs and practices to meet the needs

2. John Dewey, *Experience and Education* (New York: Henry Holt, 1938), preface.

of changing times. Our educational philosophy and practice embraced Dewey's view that moral growth is intrinsic to every learning experience.

COMMUNITY OF LEARNERS

What better way to motivate student learning than to have students and teachers learn alongside each other! Faculty do not have to have all the answers, and exhibiting their own intellectual curiosity demonstrates that learning is a rewarding, life-long endeavor. Our community of learners harked back to Dewey's belief that a democracy requires individuals to acquire a life-long habit of learning. Students and teachers had many opportunities to learn together. Each year typically began with the "unveiling" of an all-school theme, often a topic about which many of the teachers knew very little. A mathematics teacher might be uneasy working with groups of students on the theme "Poetry: Painting with Words." Or a language arts teacher might be challenged by the theme "Mathematics." (I would be remiss if I didn't mention that many of our teachers were polymaths.) Teachers and students dove into the all-school theme study together, and more often than not student and teacher learning was concurrent.

The children and adults at TPS addressed each other by their first names. This practice was a deliberate choice to engender mutual respect between adults and students and foster the feeling of being partners in learning.[3] Students tended to be less afraid to make mistakes or advocate for themselves. Many of us,

---

3. As the school community became more diverse, we became more aware of some families' discomfort with this practice. For many Black families, addressing someone as Mr., Mrs., Ms., or Miss was a sign of respect, something many whites in the South over the centuries went to great lengths to avoid in reference to Black adults. Several Asian families also struggled with the absence of traditional honorifics that show respect to elders. There is no doubt that this was a reason some families did not enroll their children at our school. This practice may warrant reconsideration.

myself included, remember our own anxiety as children of talking to "grown-ups." Some parents of prospective students worried that this practice would undermine the amount of respect
afforded to teachers, but we found that not to be the case. There
was mutual respect between teachers and students, and teachers'
authority was not undermined. The children also were aware
that different settings required different behavior; for example, visitors to the school were addressed formally (unless they
invited the children to call them by their first name).

PERSONAL CONNECTION
WITH THE TEACHER

Learning occurs when there is a human connection. We all want
to be valued, to be heard, to belong, and to identify with a sense
of purpose. Research in neuroscience shows that if emotions
are not engaged, then it is hard to make good decisions, to work
through difficult situations, to pay attention, and to remember.

As I learned from Sybil Marshall, a teacher who establishes
a strong, supportive, and respectful relationship with students
motivates them to take intellectual and creative risks to achieve
their potential. Team teaching maximizes the opportunity for
each student to be known well. In vertically grouped classrooms,
working with a student over the course of two or three years
helps teachers establish a close, long-term relationship between
the teacher and the child and the child's family.

At The Philadelphia School, one classroom teacher within a
team was responsible for the overall progress and well-being of a
student. An especially effective practice to ensure ongoing personal connection in the Middle School was the "personal journal," filled with entries by each student to their advisor, who
responded back in the journal.[4] The journal was a powerful way
advisors could stay informed of student concerns, interests, and
aspirations.

4. See Chapter 6 for more about journal writing and the special needs of
middle schoolers.

THEMATIC AND INTERDISCIPLINARY CURRICULUM

When learning is built around a central concept (Empathy), a topic (City Hall), or a question (Was Columbus a hero or villain or both?), there is purpose to the study. An interdisciplinary, thematic curriculum organizes the variety of information to be taught in a way that more closely approximates the human experience of how things happen than does the dispensing of information in isolated disciplines. It provides the focus for learning, giving purpose and meaning to the educational experience. Students know what they are learning and why, while they are learning it. A long-time TPS Middle School teacher, Emily Marston, put it aptly: "Theme is the glue that holds each discipline to another. Without it, there is less depth of understanding." An interdisciplinary approach provides more neural connections, which in turn increase the probability that material will be remembered.

The thematic curriculum at The Philadelphia School integrated the arts, literature, science, history, and mathematics, as well as Spanish and physical education when relevant. Most years began with a multi-week (or longer) all-school theme, which ranged from "City Hall" to "Empathy" to "Homer's Odyssey" to "The Olympics" to "Forests."

HUMANIZE THE CURRICULUM
AND LOGICIZE THE CHILD

One of my mantras was "humanize the curriculum and logicize the child," which I paraphrased from Dewey's *The Child and the Curriculum* (1902). Dewey wanted curriculum to be presented as a series of problems, the solutions to which called upon children to employ the methods of the scientist, the historian, and the artist. Students would construct a deeper understanding of traditional subjects and the methods used to advance them. Referring to a prior example, we might ask, "Was Columbus a hero, a villain, or both?" To find an answer, we might begin with the questions: What is a hero? Who is a hero in your immediate environment? Who were heroes in the past? How do we know who Columbus was and how did the culture of 1492 differ from that of the present-day?

TEAM TEACHING

Planning and teaching collaboratively creates a dynamic class-room. A classroom benefits from the strengths of each teacher on a team, and teachers learn by observing their teammate teaching. The interaction between team members presents an authentic, ongoing model for the students in how to relate, how to take turns, how to resolve conflicts, how to share, and how to build on the varying strengths of a collaborative group. Team teaching also enables a class to be divided into smaller groups for more individualized instruction.

Our teaching teams ranged in size from dyads to a group of six. All teachers in grades K through 8 were of equal stature (we did add a teaching assistant to each team of two Preschool teachers). This meant that they had equal voice in curriculum planning and classroom management—one more example of democracy at work in the schoolhouse.

VERTICAL GROUPING

Grouping students within a two- or three-year age span allows students to be grouped for instruction by need rather than by age.[5] For example, a student in first grade may be reading second grade material, working on first grade math, and socializing with second graders. By working with the same children over two or three years, teachers avoid the usual getting-to-know-you lag

---

5. During my time at TPS students were grouped in a variety of ways. We considered the Primary Unit to comprise kindergarten, 1st grade, and 2nd grade; Junior Unit included 3rd, 4th, and 5th grades; and Middle School was made up of 6th, 7th, and 8th grades. Preschool was added in September 2000. Grades 1 and 2 were vertically grouped; kindergarten was a stand-alone class. For many years 3rd grade was vertically grouped with 4th and 5th grades, but it became a stand-alone grade as the teachers felt that this configuration would be beneficial as 3rd grade was a time to consolidate the skills needed for 4th and 5th grades.

and the time it takes a student to internalize classroom routines; returning students can help orient the newcomers, thus recognizing their own growth over the course of the past year or two. At The Philadelphia School the students' workload was differentiated in the mixed-aged classrooms, but while there were different expectations, they remained high. Because students interacted consistently with children whose ages and abilities varied, they learned to help and be helped by other children, thereby gaining an appreciation for their own achievement and that of others.

DEVELOPMENTALLY APPROPRIATE CURRICULUM THAT IS RIGOROUS AND RELEVANT

Children are naturally inquisitive, and to further that curiosity it is critical that curriculum is developmentally appropriate, based on what a student is able to do cognitively, physically, and emotionally. An example would be any of the annual all-school themes, explored by children in all grades. During our 1987 theme celebrating the bicentennial of the U.S. Constitution, middle schoolers examined the debates surrounding the provisions of the document, while the youngest students discussed the need for rules. A focus of the theme "1972" for the Middle School was the Vietnam War, while the Junior Unit investigated the history of our school (founded in 1972).

We could train first and second graders to solve for variables such as $3 + x = 5$, but it would be meaningless to them. Instead we could lead them to understand that numbers can be broken down into individual units and combined in a variety of ways: $5 = 1 + 1 + 1 + 1 + \_\_$ or $5 = 3 + \_\_$. In this way the students are solving for an unknown variable but in a way that is less abstract and more developmentally appropriate.

HANDS-ON LEARNING

Children learn best by doing rather than by simply listening to a teacher lecture about a topic. When students are engaged with their hands and their minds to solve a problem or create something, they are more focused and motivated to learn. At TPS, children used wooden blocks, Cuisenaire rods,[6] Legos, and other concrete learning tools to help them understand concepts and move from the concrete to the abstract. They built robots, dioramas, and theatrical sets; and they assembled rock collections, planted gardens, and tended egg incubators. Our art and music programs contributed greatly as powerful hands-on avenues for children to access content. Much of this learning was collaborative, giving the students experience in working with others, listening to each other, compromising, and appreciating each other's strengths.

DIRECT EXPERIENCE AND SIMULATIONS

As I learned at the Barnes Foundation, direct experience is essential for learning. In addition to their regular trips to our country campus, students took an average of ten field trips related (and sometimes unrelated) to their classroom work each year.[7] As part of a thematic study of Ancient Greece, our Middle School students visited the Metropolitan Museum in New York to view Greek pottery; in art class, they then created their own pots decorated with an ancient design or mythological theme. Historic Philadelphia was the perfect experiential setting for our pre-teens in the Junior Unit to immerse themselves in a three-year exploration in topics in American history. One year, fourth and fifth graders each assumed the identity of members of three colonies and debated issues leading up to the Continental Congress. Another year, students created a reenactment of events

---

6. Cuisenaire rods are a collection of rectangular rods of 10 colors, each color corresponding to a different length. These manipulatives can be used to introduce, investigate, and reinforce math topics. Daniel Spielman '84, Professor of Computer Science, Mathematics, and Statistics and Data Science at Yale University, remembers that his "first experience with combinatorics was working [as a TPS student] on problems with Cuisenaire rods in the Primary Unit. They were also fun to play with."

7. For example, teachers might decide to take their students to a "once-in-a-lifetime" opportunity, such as the 1996 Cezanne exhibition at the Philadelphia Museum of Art.

surrounding the trial of Joseph Pritchard, a Quaker persecuted for his pacifist beliefs during the Revolutionary War; the reenactment was performed at early-19th-century Arch Street Meeting House.

HIGH EXPECTATIONS FOR QUALITY WORK

Caring for students means helping and seeing them thrive. Praise for mediocre work is demeaning. Teachers need to set high expectations for each student's best effort. The goal for a student should not be to receive a good grade but to make an effort to master the material. At The Philadelphia School, tests, assignments, and semester reports were ungraded. Teachers commented on student work orally or in writing; they sometimes asked a student to redo an assignment, and retests were given. Every child's work was displayed in the hallway or in the classroom as affirmation of their best effort. "Because . . . the teachers always expected the best from me," explained Amelia Lowe '99 in her graduation speech, "I have learned to expect the best from myself. I know that this will be a great help to me in high school because I won't want to settle for anything but my best."

Having high expectations does not mean that there is not a balance of process and product. Children need time to mess about, to try things out in coming to an understanding or in completing a project, but in the end there should be a product that they are proud to share. It is the teacher's role to encourage the student to move beyond the first attempts. For example, when presented with a child's painting, the teacher might ask, "What will happen if you add more color?" "Look out the window, does the sky stop at the roof top?" In reviewing a student's language arts essay, the teacher might comment, "I notice that you have used the word "nice" several times to describe characters. Can you think of other descriptive words instead of nice?"

CONSTRUCTIVIST LEARNING

Constructivism is the theory that people construct their own knowledge, developing meaning and understanding through experience and reflection. It is important that students them-selves create meaning, challenge misconceptions, and build on experience. In "Twenty-four, Forty-two, and I Love You: Keep-ing It Complex," Eleanor Duckworth explains:

> Understanding comes with being engaged in learning by grappling with complexity and playing with ideas, not having it broken down. Now do we sand away at the interesting edges of subject matter until it is so free of natural complexities, with not a crevice left as opening so the learner can only view matter as an outsider or do we let the learner struggle through their own conflicts to construct understanding?[8]

MULTIPLE PERSPECTIVES AND DIVERSITY OF OPINION

Schools must help children develop the capacity to understand competing viewpoints and belief systems; only through critical deliberation can children choose their lives' moral direction.[9] Consideration of multiple perspectives should have a place in all curricula in order to allow students to recognize and under-stand the diversity of our nation's (and other nations') communi-ties, cultures, traditions, and experiences.[10] A study of 1492, for example, would not be complete without examining the points of view of Native Americans, the European explorers, the Span-ish Crown, and the Catholic Church.

8. *Harvard Educational Review* (1991) 61 (1): 1–25. Duckworth is Pro-fessor Emerita at the Harvard School of Education.

9. Amy Gutman, *Democratic Education* (Princeton, NJ: Princeton Uni-versity Press, 1987), pp. 42–44.

10. Chris Cain '91 reflected, "TPS changed me. You must understand that I had been in sectarian schools most of my life and grew up in New Orleans. At TPS, I learned to . . . open up to new ideas and experiences. I began to question things that had been ingrained in me since birth. TPS allowed me a glimpse of other kinds of people and religions other than my own."

In preparation for the 2005–06 all-school theme "Benjamin Franklin," to coincide with Philadelphia's city-wide celebration of his 300th birthday, the faculty read several biographies and discovered that facts presented with certainty by his biographers differed from book to book. Similar discrepancies were also discovered by our students in the Franklin biographies they were reading, and this discovery led to rich discussions about the authors' differing perspectives, as well as about what makes a fact a fact.

INTELLECTUAL AND CREATIVE RISK TAKING

For as long as I can remember, students at The Philadelphia School have sung "I'm Not Perfect," a song from the 1976 album "All About Your Feelings, Songs of the Warm Fuzzy."[11] Its lyrics—which begin with "I'm not perfect and I know I never will be"—sum up the school's encouragement and celebration of intellectual and creative risk taking. TPS was a safe space for student intellectual and creative expression. As mentioned earlier, the end goal was not a good grade, so there was minimal fear of giving the wrong answer to a question or doing something wrong.[12]

THE CENTRAL ROLE OF ART, DRAMA, AND MUSIC

The arts enhance learning about the human condition and experience, as well as give students a way both to internalize content and to make a unique statement. Through the visual and performing arts, a student makes meaning of experience while determining the form and content of expression. The arts are yet another opportunity to solve problems in a unique way; it is a time when imagination is given license to fly. And for some children the arts are the main avenue toward understanding content.

---

11. Lyrics by Harriet Bird. Beloved kindergarten teacher Anne Greenwald introduced the song to TPS in the early 1980s.
12. "The Philadelphia School gave me the ability to make up my own mind—to take risks, trust my own judgment, and go for it." (Meredith Lissack '92)

Our students had regularly scheduled art, music, and drama classes, but the arts were also integrated into thematic-based classroom studies.[13] Classroom plays required the design of sets and props, Spanish classes created dioramas to demonstrate vocabulary acquisition, and science projects included drawings of rocks, leaves, invertebrates, birds, etc. Reading *Romeo and Juliet* or *The Tempest* was not enough; students performed Shakespeare, with the bard's words enhanced by musical accompaniment and dance.

OUTDOOR ENVIRONMENTAL STUDIES

Regular visits to a natural setting provide children with direct experiences that extended classroom studies in environmental, life, physical, and earth and space sciences. Time outdoors allows for exploration, observation, discovery, and reflection. Children learn to appreciate nature and become aware of their responsibility to be caretakers of the natural environment. For most of my time at The Philadelphia School, our outdoor classroom was Shelly Ridge, a Girl Scout facility located about 30 minutes by bus from our school. K–8 students spent a day each week at the 125-acre site. The many activities at the site included tending a vegetable garden, building a bridge over a stream, creek walking, orienteering, negotiating a ropes course, and journaling. Each year the entire K–8th grade community spent a day together at Shelly Ridge, working and playing in mixed-aged groups. Being able to visit the same inspiring site over many years gave the children a sense of belonging and responsibility.

KINDERGARTEN (OR PRESCHOOL)– 8TH GRADE SETTING

The experience of being among the oldest students in a school and of being a leader there can be invaluable to a young adoles-

---

13. "The fine arts are not only worthy of study in themselves but provide fascinating insight to the study of history and literature as well. TPS taught me an invaluable interdisciplinary approach that made each intellectual endeavor all the more rich." (Alicia West '97)

cent. Without the influence and pressure of high schoolers, middle school students can take part in age-appropriate activities; they can be themselves, often remaining "younger" a bit longer. Middle school students at TPS served as Student Council officers, played on interscholastic athletic teams, and were role models for younger students (who idolized them!). Unlike at many K–12 schools, our middle schoolers were taught by teachers who chose specifically to teach that age group. From time to time there were discussions among parents and the board of trustees about creating a high school; my position was that if we were to do so, the high school would have to be located at a site a good distance away from our current building.

NONSECTARIAN STANCE

The Philadelphia School was founded as a nonsectarian institution unassociated with a particular religion and not integrated within a faith community. The school did not practice any religious rituals, celebrate religious holidays, or display religious symbols. We did, however, respect religious belief and practice. We did not close school for religious holidays, but respected student and teacher absences for religious reasons. Teachers were asked not to introduce new material on days when children were out for religious observances, and accommodations were made for children in terms of project deadlines and homework.[14] We encouraged our students and their families to share their holiday traditions with classmates. Aware of the role religion has played historically around the world, we recognized that examination of religious beliefs and practices is often key to understanding the essence of a culture.

---

14. Some parents questioned this practice, often pointing out that we closed for Christmas. Winter Break did coincide with Christmas and New Year's Day, a traditional time for Americans to travel to see relatives and friends. We did not close for Good Friday or for the major Jewish holidays. Because of our team-teaching configuration, we rarely needed to hire substitutes for teachers out because of religious observance.

Because we were a nonsectarian school, parents of prospective students often asked me how or if we taught values. I explained that education of the intellect alone is insufficient, if not impossible. How do you discuss literature without facilitating a discussion about the protagonists' motivation, the impact of their status in society, or the strength or weakness of their character? How do you settle a schoolyard dispute without having established a clear expectation of fairness, kindness, and nonviolence? Intrinsic to democratic education are empathy, respect, kindness, and compassion—values modeled by our faculty each and every day.

SUSTAINED SILENT READING (SSR)

A form of school-based recreational reading, sustained silent reading helps children become not only better readers but also more avid readers. At The Philadelphia School, SSR time was also a time for faculty to read. There were actually opportunities when the school enrollment was small enough to schedule SSR for the entire school at the same time. I include sustained silent reading here because even though it is a practice widely known in educational circles, schools often discard it to make more time for STEM. I believe this is a mistake, especially in an age in which students are plugged into social media rather than into a book during their leisure time. Not only can reading be a life-long pleasure, it is critical to developing citizens with empathy, awareness of the world distant and near, and an understanding of how history informs our present and our future.[15]

STUDENT ASSESSMENT

As mentioned previously, student work was ungraded, but that did not mean that we did not assess student progress. Assess-

---

15. Jon Levy '88 commented in a 2022 alumni survey that he read for pleasure "a great deal" and that the "practice of SSR has always stayed with me."

ment came in a variety of forms. Mastery of material could be easily discerned in classroom discussions and project work. The expressive delivery of lines in a Middle School performance of *Julius Caesar* would reveal how much a student understood Shakespeare's text. By writing a play about a "fairer America," third graders revealed how well they understood such content as the Emancipation Proclamation, the civil rights movement, immigration, and unionization. For first and second graders, the experience of giving older students a guided tour of their classrooms during their Primary Unit "theme celebration" demonstrated to others—and to themselves—all that they had learned during their theme study.

We did minimal testing. Teacher-designed tests gave immediate feedback to teachers and students about progress toward goals. Older students were encouraged to take retests, since the purpose of the test for the student was to monitor progress and gain understanding, not to achieve a grade. Teachers changed lessons or assisted individual students to suit the degree of mastery of content or skills revealed by the test results.

We used standardized tests for specific purposes.[16] We administered the Boehm National Normed Tests for Language Acquisition in kindergarten as a pre-and post-test of understanding of basic concepts that are essential for success in school, such as first/last, top/bottom, left/right, and up/down. Test results were a guide for instruction and an indicator of the need for extra attention for lower-scoring students. Botel Reading Milestone Tests served as diagnostic screens to determine the phonetic skills and reading instructional levels of all students. Given each year in the fall and spring, the Botels were used to check for progress over time and to guide student grouping for lan-

---

16. I think I may have shocked the TPS parent community in 2006, when I wrote a somewhat scathing article entitled "When Child Abuse Is Mandatory" in response to the high-stakes testing that had been (and continues to be) offered by politicians as the solution to improve learning and teaching in our nation's public schools.

guage arts instruction. Results were used, together with teacher observation and other classroom measures, as part of a running record. Basically multiple-choice vocabulary tests, the Botels related well with reading level in the early grades but were not as valid in the middle school, where we relied more on teacher observation and student performance.

We also gave Education Records Bureau (ERB)[17] standardized tests in fourth, fifth, and seventh grades in the spring. We devoted minimal time to test prep. Knowing at the time that standardized testing was in the children's futures for high school and college admission, we felt we had to give them the experience of answering multiple-choice questions and filling in the bubble sheets (now probably a thing of the past). The tests can also be a measure of program effectiveness as they gauge student, grade, and school achievement compared to norm groups (national, suburban, and independent schools over the previous three years for a specific grade).

We hand-scored parts of the test for fourth graders and shared the results with teachers and, if they asked, parents. The scores were not part of a student's record because, for us, the primary use was to look for discrepancies between teacher assessments and test results and to give students practice with the format and answer sheet. Test results for fifth and seventh graders were shared with parents at a conference with me and/or the advisor. We also shared the results with the seventh graders; we were reluctant to share them earlier because we did not want to create undue test anxiety. Because standardized test scores were required by public magnet and independent schools as part of the admissions process, some practice and familiarity were important.

---

17. The Education Records Bureau has renamed its testing products since I left TPS. The tests are designed to measure ability in verbal and quantitative reasoning and achievement in vocabulary, reading comprehension, writing mechanics, writing concepts and skills, and mathematics. For more information, go to https://erblearn.org/.

We carefully reviewed ERB results, especially item analysis, to measure our program effectiveness. If a large percentage (over 60%) of students answered a question incorrectly, we looked at what the content was and determined whether it was important content to teach at a particular grade level, if at all.

CHAPTER 3

Finding the Right People

*Teaching might even be the greatest of the arts since the
medium is the human mind and spirit.*

John Steinbeck

*There is no recipe to be a great teacher, that's
what is unique about them.*

Professor Robert Sternberg, Cornell University

I WAS FORTUNATE to lead a school that was on a growth
trajectory in terms of enrollment throughout my tenure. This
meant that I had the opportunity to hire many extraordinary
teachers over the years. Our program attracted gifted individuals who were life-long learners, who thrived in an intellectual
environment, who relished creating content and lessons, who
liked a challenge, and who believed that teaching was a calling.
They respected and loved children as learners. They believed in
progressive educational philosophy. Teaching at The Philadelphia School meant working in a multi-grade setting with a team
or partner; this itself required flexibility, hard work, a sense of
humor, and patience. Our teachers were good listeners, taskmas-
ters, and performers.

Before describing faculty recruitment, I want to emphasize
that our salary scale was the same for preschool teachers as for
middle school faculty. Teachers of art, music, physical education, and Spanish were also paid on the same salary scale. Unfor-

tunately, this pay equity is uncharacteristic in many schools. Devaluing and underpaying the teachers of our youngest students undermine the foundation of American public, parochial, and independent schooling. I also tried to offer only full-time positions, wanting to make sure teachers had financial stability and benefits.

In recruiting faculty, I went well beyond looking at cover letters, resumés, grade point averages, and recommendations. Promising candidates were invited to the school to teach a lesson. In a few cases, I was able to observe candidates in their current classrooms rather than asking them to present a lesson in a totally unfamiliar environment with children they did not know. After a favorable observation, I would stroll through our school with the candidate and discuss what they saw. I was looking to discern their interest and understanding of what was occurring in the classrooms and what was displayed in the hallways. I was especially interested in what they were reading, what their favorite books for children were, and what courses they took in college. A wide variety of university course selections reflected curiosity beyond their principal area of study—oftentimes this revealed a versatile, well-rounded person. If an applicant seemed like a viable candidate, they then spent time with the team with whom they would be working. Because teaming was critical to the mission of the school, a candidate was hired only if the team was enthusiastic about the individual.

Many of the teachers I hired did not have degrees in education—and some had little teaching experience. As someone who holds an Ed.D., I do value teaching experience and coursework in pedagogy. However, a person who lacks conventional prerequisites but possesses a passion for their discipline often has an innate understanding of what works. And when teaching thematically, a teacher needs to be open to new areas of study—here is where intellectual curiosity is essential. If I had hired only individuals with teaching experience and with degrees in education, our students would have missed working with several hugely inspiring teachers. Key to orienting new faculty members, especially those new to teaching, was our team-teaching structure—learning by doing with the guidance of their exceptional colleagues.

Here are a few examples of unconventional hires. One of the earliest was a music teacher with no teaching experience. A harpsichordist with equal comfort on the piano, Marcia Kravis was a brilliant musician who had recently returned to Philadelphia after time in Berkeley, CA. During our interview, it was clear to me that she was sincerely interested in learning about the Orff instruments and Kodaly method we used for teaching music. It was apparent that she belonged in a community of learners.

Throughout Marcia's many years at TPS, this brilliant musician became not only an excellent music teacher but also an inspired producer of student drama and opera. Her collaborative, thematic work with classroom teachers was exceptional, and entering her classroom was for me always a magical experience, seeing the children engaged in whatever they were working on—a composition, an ensemble piece, or a performance.

Had I not hired this extraordinary teacher because of a lack of formal credentials, what a loss this would have been for hundreds of students who learned music theory, sang in chorus, and performed in the musicals she directed (and for which she often wrote the music and lyrics) in such city venues as the Please Touch Museum, the Plays & Players Theatre, the Gershman YMHA, and the Port of History Museum.

Another nontraditional addition to the faculty was also a musician, a solo violist who had sent in a resumé and cover letter to apply to teach music. Aaron Picht had experience teaching individual students but not groups. Because the school did not have current openings, I almost put his resumé aside, perhaps for another time. However, his musical accomplishments were so remarkable that I decided to meet him. I learned that his wife, a violinist, had been hired by the Philadelphia Orchestra, so he was looking to find work in music in the Philadelphia area. He had given up playing professionally and was looking for teaching opportunities. By the end of our conversation, I was not only impressed with Aaron's musical background but also with his humble demeanor and his intellectual heft. And, perhaps somewhat selfishly, I saw that he just might be the person to bring to fruition my dream of a small orchestra for the school. I offered Aaron the opportunity to teach violin in our after-school music program; and when a faculty position opened up a year or two later, he became a valuable full-time teacher, as well as conductor of two string ensembles, at the school. All of this came about from taking the time to consider more than his resumé. (I am still waiting for a full orchestra!)

An especially interesting and somewhat "risky" hire was a woman who had very little teaching experience beyond teaching music lessons in our after-school program. The risk was that she was hired to team teach first and second grade, where teaching early reading and math was critical. But I had gotten to know Kit Mitchell over the years—her daughter was enrolled at the school—and she was an active parent volunteer in support of a variety of school programs. I decided that her own high school education at a progressive boarding school in Vermont, where students were required to learn by doing and to be self-motivated, had been the perfect training ground to learn from her new teammate in the Primary Unit. And so it was. Kit became an outstanding teacher, loved by her students and their parents. Her training in family therapy at Bryn Mawr College was also valuable in working with families, her teaching team, and other colleagues.

A final example of one of my non-traditional hires was also a musician, originally from Chile, who had performed at TPS with his band from time to time in support of our Spanish program.[1] A former member of a Chilean pop group, Marco Velis had left Chile in his last year of studying music education at the Instituto Pedagogico de la Universidad de Chile. He completed his music studies at Berklee College in Boston. In 1992, we had

1. There seems to be a theme here, perhaps showing some personal bias as I am the parent of a classically trained, professional musician!

an immediate opening for a Spanish teacher, and as the number of middle schoolers was expected to grow in the coming years, I needed to plan to staff an additional theme teacher/advisor. Learning that history teaching was part of this candidate's family legacy—his father was a history teacher in Chile—I was confident that Marco could ultimately become both a Spanish and theme teacher. He would bring a South American perspective to the theme studies and integrate thematic topics into his Spanish language classes. Still teaching at The Philadelphia School long after I left, he continues to masterfully bring music, Spanish culture and history, and compassion into his classroom.

I am proud of assembling and supporting a dynamic faculty of hard-working, smart, caring, and sometimes quirky individuals who could not have been better models for the children they taught and advised. The attributes of our master teachers were many—but, at the core, there was always something wonderfully magical and mysteriously indefinable.

CHAPTER 4

Connecting with Faculty

I define connection as the energy that exists between people when they feel seen, heard, and valued; when they give and receive without judgment; and when they derive sustenance and strength from the relationship.

Professor Brené Brown, University of Houston

As MENTIONED EARLIER, learning occurs best when there is a human connection. We all want to be valued, to be heard, to belong, and to identify with a sense of purpose. As a community of learners, it was important that our teachers had a strong sense of connection with me, with each other, and with students and parents. I worked to find ways to foster these connections, as well as connections between the school and the wider community.

Teaching, although immensely rewarding, is a difficult job. My prior years of teaching children in a wide range of grades—from second to eleventh—enabled me to connect to the faculty and understand their challenges. As a teacher, I had felt validated when my work was recognized. When teachers feel appreciated, valued, and heard, they are more likely to do the same with their students. I believe it was clear to the teachers that I was truly invested in their success, their teaching, and their professional development.

I like to think of my management style as "walking around."

I visited almost every classroom nearly every day, taking in what was happening, noting the engagement of the students, and observing the lesson. If possible, while I was there, I would mention something positive that I had noticed or ask about the teacher's family or a project they were working on.[1] On occasion I would drop a note in their mailbox or mention something about the class I visited during our faculty and staff meeting. I frequently attended team meetings, primarily to listen but occasionally to raise an issue or comment on curricular decisions. I was always available if a teacher wanted a one-on-one meeting; my office door was always open. I would occasionally schedule a formal observation of a lesson and meet with the teacher to discuss that lesson, but this was not related to evaluation.

From time to time, faculty members, usually from each unit, took part in study groups. Topics ranged from the U.S. Constitution to Howard Gardner's theory of multiple intelligences. I tried to be a regular participant, not only because I was interested in the content but also because I wanted to demonstrate my support for the teachers as they wrestled with new material and new ideas to develop curricula for their students.

DISTRIBUTED LEADERSHIP

The Philadelphia School had a flat organizational structure with no bureaucracy and with distributed leadership; expertise and responsibilities were stretched over people in different roles rather than divided among them.[2] This approach had many advantages, the primary one being the avoidance of a hierarchi-

---

1. "I remember with good thoughts the times you would walk into my fourth-grade math class-that tiny room in Junior Unit with all the blackboards. You would just get yourself between a group of students as they worked on the board and start asking questions. I felt honored and proud when you would visit my classroom. I felt supported by you, and you gave me the courage to explore my teaching." (Paul De Angelis, Junior Unit teacher)

2. James P. Spillane, Richard Halverson, and John B. Diamond, "Distributed Leadership: Toward a Theory of School Leadership," *Journal of Curriculum Studies*, January 2004, 36(1):3–34.

cal organization that might discourage independence, innovation, and risk taking on the part of the faculty and staff. There were no division heads, deans of students, or supervisors.

Because the ratio of students to fully qualified teachers was approximately eleven or twelve to one, teachers were able to assume responsibilities that were usually assumed at other schools by teaching assistants, curriculum specialists, or division directors. Our teachers selected curriculum and materials, arranged for substitutes, and managed their own professional development. In this way, faculty could decide what best met the needs of their classrooms and students.

This did not mean there was no oversight. Teams met with me when deciding on or changing themes, and my approval was required for field trips and most purchases (a teacher could make small purchases on their own, knowing that they would be reimbursed without question). Teachers ordered some books and materials to begin the year, and they could buy what they needed as the school year unfolded. It seemed counterproductive to give teachers a specific amount of funds at the start of the school year. Teachers might feel the need to spend that amount before they knew what they would require. Or they might withhold spending their budgeted amount for fear of unexpected needs or opportunities later in the school year. It was never completely predictable what direction a unit theme might take, even though the topic had been decided in the previous spring. We did not know what aspect of the theme would be particularly interesting to the children and what unanticipated questions might arise. For example, a study of Benjamin Franklin could result in questions about electricity or the Constitution—leading to field trips to the Franklin Institute and the National Constitution Center.

CONTRACT TALKS

In the spring I would meet with each teacher (and administrative staff member) individually to talk about renewing the yearly contract. These talks included determining the extent to which a teacher had met their goals, setting new goals, and reviewing the teacher's self-evaluation. In addition to receiving a salary raise, a teacher might be qualified to receive a bonus that was cumulative, not just a one-year addition. The bonus recognized not only extraordinary performance of tasks required by contract but also activities or initiatives not explicitly covered by contract, such as

- completing workshops or courses to improve practice
- testing prospective students for admission
- organizing all-school initiatives and events (for example, Student Council, Thanksgiving Feast, All-School Theme Celebration)
- working with a student teacher or training a new team member
- attending family and student activities outside of the normal school day (for example, the annual picnic, fund-raising events, and Saturday orientations to the nature center)
- attending and presenting at admissions open houses and fairs
- participating in a study group
- taking on a leadership role in thematic or environmental education
- serving as a team leader (Team leaders attended a monthly meeting with me, where I shared mostly administrative information that they, in turn, would relate to their teams. This cut down on the number of meetings teachers needed to attend.)
- planning and facilitating initiatives that contributed to the greater good, for example, food drives for local shelters and read-a-thons to raise funds for regional and international causes

It was rare that a teacher did not receive a bonus. Teachers who did not receive one generally understood that they were not a good fit for the school and sought employment elsewhere.

DISTRIBUTED LEADERSHIP BEYOND FACULTY

For me, prioritizing faculty was key to a successful school. Managing by walking around took time and was only possible by applying the idea of distributed leadership to the school's administrative staff,[3] Board of Trustees, and parents' association. As a school leader, I was an educator first and foremost, and their support of the school's mission was critical. I wanted the school to function without a bureaucratic structure, again, without supervisors between myself and the teachers. We had the benefit of an administrative staff, Board of Trustees, and parent volunteers who understood that their role was to help support the work that was being done by teachers. The resulting operational economies allowed us to afford to maintain a ratio of two full-time teachers per twenty-four students.

ADMINISTRATIVE STAFF[4]

Our lean, hard-working administrative staff, which numbered 9 (including me) in my last year when student enrollment was 371, was given the responsibility, authority, and autonomy to do or oversee many of the tasks often done or closely supervised by a head of school. I met with them as needed and was kept abreast of how things were going, but I did not micromanage. I trusted my staff.

Each staff member knew that their job was to assist the faculty and that the education of children was at the center of

3. I am using the term "administrative staff" here, although I do not recall ever using it during my tenure at The Philadelphia School. We did not use the term "administration" either. We were "faculty and staff." There was no distinction between administration and faculty as seen in most schools; perhaps that was a nod to a democratic resistance to hierarchy. One senior staff member recalls simply telling people that she "worked in the office."

4. Up until about 2000, the administrative staff consisted of the head of school, the admissions director, the development director, the business manager, a part-time bookkeeper, and the school secretary. We later added a receptionist, a communications director, and assistants helping out in admission, development, and finance.

everything we did. If a teacher needed to use a copier that was in the midst of producing 500 fund-raising letters, staff knew to "step away from the machine" or offer to do the copying for the teacher. Staff also understood that their work had to be of the highest quality as it needed to reflect the excellence of our faculty and school. They worked collaboratively, balanced each other's strengths and weaknesses, and cared deeply about their work and the school. (Dewey would have been delighted.)

Office staff also wore multiple hats. The business manager not only was responsible for billing and receipts but also oversaw the management of the plant. The director of admissions recruited and welcomed new students and families, as well as served as the school's liaison to the parents' association. For many years, the director of development not only managed fund-raising campaigns and events but was also responsible for internal and external communications and assisted me on special projects. Office staff also had regular lunch and recess duty, participated in all-school events and outings, and attended all faculty meetings regardless of topic (we called them "faculty and staff meetings"). I encouraged staff to share their own interests with students, and several led or coached after-school activities (the school secretary taught cheerleading, and our building manager was our soccer coach), taught middle school mini-courses (the director of development taught Russian), and helped teachers find speakers related to classroom studies.

BOARD OF TRUSTEES

Our Board of Trustees, composed mainly of current and former TPS parents, supported the school's philosophy and mission. Trustees provided wealth, wisdom, and work: they raised money, donated their professional expertise (legal, architectural, financial, technological), oversaw capital projects, researched salary structures, established policies (for example, parental leave and salary scale), and undertook strategic planning. Their purview did not include educational decisions. My team could not have accomplished what we did without their dedication and work.

I began each board meeting with a summary of curricular activities, faculty achievements, and student progress. My goal was not only to keep trustees informed but to ground their decision-making in the school's core values. My staff proposed the budget for the coming school year—subject to board approval— and the board set tuition increases accordingly. I provided the context in which board members could best perform their fiduciary duty to act in the interests of the school and those it served.

PARENTS ASSOCIATION

An active and supportive group of parent volunteers was vital throughout the school year in allowing me and my staff to attend to the needs of teachers and students. I took part in their monthly meetings, along with one or two of my staff. The parents association (TPSA, short for The Philadelphia School Association) took the lead on many school events, ranging from organizing Grandparents Day and the Book Fair to baking lasagnas for the Thanksgiving Feast to providing refreshments on Conference Days and Graduation Day. Their support was not only invaluable in terms of helping a lean staff but also expressed to the faculty a commitment to the school's culture and mission.

TEACHER FEEDBACK

After Graduation Day in June, teachers and staff participated in a week-long in-service to close the year and to prepare for the next. During in-service we held small-group meetings made up of ten teachers and staff members, with each group including teachers from each grade. Participants were asked not to discuss their meeting prior to completion of all the meetings, so that results were not influenced by views expressed in prior gatherings. Each group listed what made the year especially good and then listed problems. Group members were asked not to discuss or try to find solutions for problems that were mentioned, which could be anything from a leaking drinking fountain to the absence of parental leave. I took notes and then prepared a master list that I presented to the faculty and staff at our two-week in-service in late August. During that session, we attempted to solve out-standing problems (some building maintenance problems would have been corrected during the summer). Major policy issues, such as parental leave, were discussed with the Board of Trust-ees and often, as in this case, corrected. Individual or team prob-lems would be addressed during the school year as they arose.

The end-of-year group meetings revealed what mattered most to the faculty and staff. They gave me a window into the morale of faculty and staff, and they showed them that I wanted to hear their voices and respond to their concerns. For example, in June 2002 the meetings yielded 95 positive comments: 18 praised events that encouraged community participation ("All-School Shelly Ridge Day was great. It created a sense of community early in the year." "The Odyssey read-a-loud brought the school together in a beautiful way, and it was terrific to have the vari-ety of readers. Can we do something like this next year?"); 31 responses expressed appreciation of individual contributions to the successful running of the school ("Our building manager, Brian, is kind, thoughtful, funny, anticipates needs of the faculty like spotlights and wheels on the spacecraft for Mission to Mars, even when asked at the last minute." "Maria, her after-school Latin dance was great." "Abbie appreciated the collaboration with the staff as we created teams around vulnerable children.); another 20 comments conveyed appreciation of academic pro-grams ("The writing curriculum that Susan worked on, includ-ing exploring crafting techniques of various authors." "The Space Mission was very exciting and more parent and audience friendly." "Loved the Jackson Pollock project and paintings in the entrance."); the remaining 26 positive comments expressed appreciation for changes that made the lives of the faculty eas-ier (for example, allotting more time for writing student progress reports and constructing a movable wall between the two kin-dergarten classes).

The 2002 wrap-up meetings also identified 95 problems, issues, and questions. Many of the requests for logistical changes could be solved once the people involved were aware: "Friday notes often did not make it to the correspondence notebook."[5] Requests for ease and comfort were often corrected: "Can we have water as an option in the staff soda machine?" "Younger children can't open the latch on some bathroom stalls; the latches need to be lower."

Sharing these basically minor issues made the community aware of how each of us could make things just a bit more comfortable. Some issues were not fixable because they involved requests for more time with students and there were conflicting interests. One request was from the art department, which wanted double periods for middle school students. Lynn Paige, the designer of our outstanding art curriculum, wrote the following to me:

> I know you have always supported a strong art program as being an important part of the Middle School schedule, but I don't know if you realize how important this is to the current 8th grade class. Chris comes in to see me daily and literally begged me to let him take linoleum and tools with him to Atlantic City so he wouldn't lose "the flow." Zamira, Katherine, Aris, and Rachel begged me to let them take work home, which I did. Steve, Rick, and Ian keep asking me for extra time, recess, anything. I am giving them a more sophisticated curriculum than they had in the early grades; it requires more complicated processes. And you need more time to do the work than a 40-minute period. I will, of course, go along with whatever constraints must occur in the schedule but feel very sad about losing my momentum with the eighth grade and sadder still that they cannot have this time which is so valuable to them."

To accommodate this request, another teacher would have had to give up time with the same students. The Middle School

---

5. Prior to going primarily digital, we kept a binder that contained, in chronological order, all communications to parents.

team and the art teachers met to try to find a solution, asking the question, What is best for the students? As I recall, there was a less than satisfactory resolution. But it certainly impressed and pleased me that the teachers were advocating for more teaching time—not less!

Although I could not accommodate every teacher need or request, I like to think that faculty knew that I tried to support them in any way feasible. Underlying all my interactions with teachers was a desire to let them know that I respected them, cared about them, and trusted them.

CHAPTER 5

Faculty Connecting
with Each Other

*A better vision for a workplace is a community—a place where
people bond around shared values, feel valued as human
beings, and have a voice in decisions that affect them.*

Professor Adam Grant, Wharton School

WALKING IN THE CITY these days, with the proliferation of
cell phones, it quickly becomes obvious that people need connection. The classroom can be a lonely place for a teacher. I
wanted to create not only a collegial atmosphere within the individual classrooms but across the school. This was accomplished
in several ways.

TEAM TEACHING

Watching teaching teams work together was sometimes like
watching a ballet. Often a teaching team was a perfect balance
of talents and skills. We had three vertically grouped first and
second grade classrooms, each team-taught by two teachers.
These six classroom teachers planned together, with each of
them taking the lead in an area of particular strength or interest.
One classroom had both a reading and a mathematics specialist (although both taught all subjects), and these two teachers brought their expertise to the entire unit. Another teacher

took the lead in planning writing, and others focused on science or theme.

Team teaching had numerous benefits. For example, in each of our Primary Unit classrooms, one teacher led the morning meeting, usually on a rotating schedule, while the other sat next to a child who needed attention or moved about to help students attend. A student's progress can be better assessed when two or more teachers are observing and working with the child. When team members can share responsibility of working with a child who is experiencing difficulties, it is beneficial to both the teachers and the student.

Our Junior Unit (grades 3–5) and Middle School (grades 6–8) were team-taught by a group of teachers ranging in number from three to six. During morning meetings, each teacher seamlessly took a turn to discuss the day's schedule or remind students of upcoming events or trips. Planning and teaching with a large team could be challenging, but putting several bright, creative teachers together resulted in engaging and effective learning experiences for the students.

Team teaching was intrinsically a form of professional development. Teachers learned from each other. The practice of even the most experienced teachers was enhanced by observing, collaborating with, and planning with colleagues. Teachers were expected to continue growing as educators.

Major advantages from an institutional point of view are continuity of program and retention of institutional memory. If one member of the team leaves at the end of the year, the teacher(s) who return in the fall can maintain routines and can help orient the new partner; in a vertically grouped classroom, this means one or more of the teachers already know the returning students.

Finally, the team-teaching model is a powerful, daily model for children of what makes for a democratic community: individuals working respectfully together, helping each other, listening to each other, taking turns, compromising, and being accountable to one another.

PROGRAM DEVELOPMENT

As mentioned previously, The Philadelphia School faculty wrote curricula, planned thematic units, and worked on philosophy. No two years were alike in our classrooms. The all-school theme changed every year, requiring new lessons, field trips, and guest presenters. From third grade on up, the curriculum consisted of a three-year rotation; that meant that topics were revisited by teachers (including specialists)[1] every three years. Our first and second grade classrooms had a two-year science rotation. Each year's all-school theme was determined in the preceding spring by a faculty and staff vote that followed a day of lively debate and discussion.

I expected teachers to develop the programs needed by their students. Content could be determined by a teacher's passion (for example, the Mission to Mars program in the Junior Unit), by student interest (for example, the selection by vote of the animal to study in kindergarten), or by current events (for example, the 20th anniversary of Earth Day). This approach made for a dynamic and rewarding collaborative experience for the teachers, admittedly one that required a great deal of work.

SUMMER READING

Students were not the only members of our school community who were assigned summer reading. Faculty and staff had a summer assignment as well. We discussed the assigned book when we returned for our two-week in-service after the summer break, usually on our first day of meetings held at my home. This practice was an effective way to involve new colleagues, and it gave all of us an authentic and meaningful way to interact and share common values and language.

---

1. Instead of having to create separate lessons for 6th, 7th, and 8th graders, specialists could prepare a strong theme-related curriculum for all three grades since they all had the same thematic curriculum in a given year. For example, when the students were studying the medieval period, they all worked on medieval mosaics in art class and Gregorian chants in chorus.

We read a wide variety of books. Some were chosen in preparation for the all-school theme; for example, we read *Lost Child in the Woods* by Richard Louv to prepare for our "Forest" theme, and we read *The Way it Was: 1876* by Suzanne Hilton in preparation for the theme "Child Times" (an exploration of childhood in the United States). Books related to educational philosophy included *Experiment in Education* by Sybil Marshall and *The End of Education* by Neil Postman. Selections related to issues of race and social injustice included *Black Ice* by Lorene Cary, *Learning to Bow* by Bruce S. Feiler, *Savage Inequalities* by Jonathan Kozol, and *There Are No Children Here* by Alex Kotlowitz. Titles related to practice included *Bird by Bird* by Anne Lamont, *Teaching School* by Eric W. Johnson, and *Blessings of a Skinned Knee* by Wendy Mogel.

FACULTY AND STAFF MEETINGS

Faculty and staff were required to attend bi-weekly 75-minute meetings after school on Wednesdays. I always attended the meetings and usually led them. We kept announcements to a minimum, reserving them for unit and office meetings.[2] Instead we discussed ideas and philosophy, shared classroom experiments and curricula, and celebrated birthdays and other life events. As mentioned earlier, administrative staff was expected to attend all meetings—I wanted everyone to know what was going on in the school. And I wanted staff to understand how much more there was to teaching than simply presenting a lesson.

The content of faculty meetings varied according to the needs of the teachers. For example, we spent several meetings discussing Howard Gardner's book *Frames of Mind: The Theory of Multiple Intelligences*. As the product of his research, Gardner

---

2. Each teacher had one planning period a day as well as at least two weekly unit meetings, at which time, in addition to planning, individual student issues were discussed. Office meetings were less frequent, often occurring before an important event or board meeting.

identified seven distinct intellectual competencies—linguistic, logical-mathematical, spatial, musical, bodily kinesthetic, interpersonal, and intrapersonal. According to Gardner, every human being can develop each of these intelligences, although it is unlikely that an individual will develop them in equal measure. At our faculty and staff meeting, we discussed how we could be sure that we were giving students opportunities to experience all these competencies and how we could help students use one or more of the elevated levels of intelligence in learning.

Some meetings were devoted to curriculum development. Looking at the mathematics, language arts, or science curriculum, teachers worked in groups across grades in order to become aware of what preceded their grade and what the students needed to master for the grade ahead. Other meetings were devoted to teacher presentations of a new approach, a new project, or what was happening in that unit.

My doctoral dissertation (2006) grew out of then-new brain research on attention and related subjects. I wanted the faculty to become aware of research findings that could be applied in the classroom. To do this I set up an experiment that I hoped would bring the subject to life and, since the topic was attention, captured the attention of my audience! In a subsequent chapter I will describe the meetings devoted to that experiment and its follow-up in a middle school classroom.

ADDITIONAL OPPORTUNITIES FOR FACULTY CONNECTION

By contract, faculty were expected to arrive 30 minutes before classes began at 8:20am and to stay 30 minutes after student dismissal at 3:20pm. This ensured that there was time to talk with teammates or, occasionally, meet with students or parents. Each Wednesday, teachers remained at school until 5:20pm for team meetings or full faculty and staff meetings. It was not uncommon for teachers to stay late to work on planning. The school building remained open until 6:00pm to accommodate afterschool programs, including childcare, clubs, sports, and individual and group music lessons.³ Several teachers taught in these programs, and they became acquainted not only with students they did not teach during the day but also with faculty members from different classrooms.

FACULTY AND STAFF PARTNERSHIP

It was important to me that administrative staff viewed themselves as partners in the education of our students. This was essential to achieve our goal of fostering a sense of responsibility for all students. Staff members were assigned lunch and recess duty, as well as yard duty in the morning or afternoon. Students knew all the adults in the building, including office and facilities staff.

Whether in hallways, in the schoolyard, or on the playground, staff were ready to attend to a student need or to give a behavior reminder, such as a simple "no running in the hallway." If staff overheard or saw something especially positive or troubling, we would notify the advisor of the student involved. A notebook, the "alert notebook," was kept in the office, where teachers and staff could briefly record information of which everyone needed to be aware, such as a death or illness in the family that might affect the behavior or performance of a child. If there was a new entry, the blackboard that listed events of the week would be marked with a red check, notifying faculty and staff to check the alert notebook. Through this practice we tried to discourage the attitude "not my job or not my kids," and we were able to connect with the community in a compassionate way. A parent whose father had died wrote to me that he

> was surprised to receive such a note [condolence from a faculty member] simply because I wouldn't have thought

3. The After School Enrichment Program (ASEP) was created when we realized the increasing number of latch-key children (some actually wearing keys on strings around their necks) who were going home to empty houses because their parents were at work. The program provided a home-like environment for students and included art projects, cooking, board games, outdoor play, and impromptu play with friends.

you knew. But, reflecting upon this, I realized that you and the faculty and staff at TPS have made it even more of a true community than I had realized. Thank you again for your thoughtfulness and compassion.

Teachers are the intellect, heart, and soul of an educational program. But they can only do their work if they are part of a community that trusts, respects, and appreciates their professionalism.

CHAPTER 6

Connecting with Students

*Good teachers don't approach a child of this age with
overzealousness or with destructive conscientiousness.
They're not drill-masters in the military or floor
managers in a productive system. They are specialists
in opening small packages. They give the string a
tug but do it carefully. They don't yet know what's
in the box. They don't know if it's breakable.*

Jonathan Kozol (*Ordinary Resurrections:
Children in the Years of Hope*)

As a school leader, I visited classrooms often, noticing
what the children were working on and sometimes taking part
in their class activities.[1] I attended all thematic celebrations,
plays, and musical performances, as well as many sports events.
At the end of each school day, I stood at the exit and shook every
student's hand. (Later, when the flu and other viruses became
an issue, I substituted a nod or tap on the shoulder for a hand-
shake.) The younger students often shared something important that happened during the day, where they were going after
school, or just something that was on their minds. One of my
favorite memories was a comment made by a five-year-old on the
way out the door. "Sandy, Sandy," she joyfully shouted, "Guess

---

1. I attended Spanish class with a group of students as they progressed
from 1st through 4th grade.

what happened to my parents!" I answered, "They are going on a vacation?" "No," she shouted, proudly announcing, "They got a new mattress!" I loved this comment because we educators never knew what was foremost in these wonderful minds. Part of the beauty of working with young children is experiencing the world as they do, seeing things for the first time in new and original ways.

There is nothing more important in a school than the moment-to-moment interaction between a student and a teacher. What are the attributes of a gifted teacher that make those moments so meaningful? A gifted teacher has a sense of humor, a profound respect for childhood, and a perceptive intuition. Equally important is being knowledgeable about craft and subject matter. Gifted teachers have an extraordinary ability to connect the child's experience with the intellectual content being taught, even when at first glance a connection may seem a stretch—for example, teaching Homer's *Odyssey* to kindergartners, the United States Constitution to fourth and fifth graders, and Shakespeare's *Julius Caesar* to middle schoolers.

Great teachers are fearless and creative in the face of intellectual challenges in shaping content. To enhance classroom and all-school themes, our teachers took it upon themselves to write plays and musicals for student performance. And these endeavors were mighty ambitious, for example, an all-school musical about the 1787 Constitutional Convention and a Primary Unit musical about Manjiro, the first person from Japan to visit the United States.[2] Classroom teachers collaborated with the music department to help first and second graders write operas based on the work of Picasso and on the children's book *Swimmy* by Leo Lionni. A middle school science teacher went above and beyond

2. *The Adventures of Manjiro* was commissioned by the Rosenbach Museum & Library in conjunction with its exhibition of Manjiro's illustrated manuscript. After performances in Philadelphia, the school received an invitation to perform the play in Manjiro's hometown of Kochi, Japan, and a small troupe of our older students flew to Kochi, where they performed the musical at three elementary schools.

to help students create costumes and build stilts to take part in the city's celebration of the 20th anniversary of Earth Day.

Maximizing connections between students and teachers was taken into consideration in all aspects of our program. These connections promoted individual attention and ensured that every child was known by faculty and staff members throughout the school. The evolving developmental needs of children, as they grow from preschoolers to eighth graders, were at the center of an educational program that addressed their social-emotional, intellectual, and physical needs. Key was a close relationship between teachers and students. Small-group and individual instruction was our goal. I believe we had a school structure, classroom design solutions, and a schedule that were optimal for addressing the needs of children as they made their journey from preschoolers through graduating eighth graders.

I supported the basic structure of the classrooms I had inherited. The model was ungraded and vertically grouped, with students separated into three units. Initially, Primary Unit consisted of grades K–2; Junior Unit, 3–5; and Middle School, 6–8. A class of 18–24 students was taught by two teachers in each of the Primary Unit rooms. The vertically grouped Junior Unit was taught by a team of three to seven teachers, and the vertically grouped Middle School by a team of four to six. Kindergarten and third grade each eventually became a one-year program; this change was initiated by the teachers, who recognized the need for these children to consolidate skills before moving into a more demanding program. Preschool was added in 2000 as a two-year program with 3- and 4-year-olds.[3] As enrollment grew throughout the school, we increased staffing accordingly to maintain small-group instruction.

The principle underlying vertical grouping—the two- or three-year duration of a child's tenure in the same classroom—was that students, regardless of their designated grade, would be able

---

3. Shortly after my departure from TPS, the preschool became a one-year program for 4-year-olds.

to work at the level of which they were capable. That level was not so easy that a student was bored or so difficult that a student stopped engaging with the material. We wanted to create some tension, a mild degree of anxiety, so that when difficult work was tackled and mastered it would result in a growing willingness to approach difficult topics and content. Joy in learning was heightened by an authentic sense of achievement.

Our multi-year classrooms created a more family-like atmosphere, where older students modeled the behaviors required for a well-managed classroom and younger students would feel supported. In addition, in the second and third years, teachers already knew each returning student, saving valuable getting-to-know-you time at the beginning of the second or third year. Returning students could also help orient incoming younger classmates. Vertical grouping was also an advantage in that teachers could work with their students' parents over a two- or three-year period. Single-year kindergarten and third grade were exceptions, but their low student-teacher ratio, with two classroom teachers, ensured that students were well supported and known.

Students in the Junior Unit and Middle School were assigned one of their classroom teachers as an advisor. Advisor assignment was made after careful consideration during June in-service, with a student's current teachers making recommendations for the next year's advisor. The bond between student and advisor was generally strong, with each knowing the other very well. Over the two or three years that a child was in a unit, the advisor was responsible for assuring that the student was progressing academically and managing emotionally and socially. The advisor was the main contact for parents throughout the school year and met with parents in the fall and spring for conferences.

SCHEDULE AND SPACE

Schedule and space considerations responded to an educational program carefully designed to meet the needs of our children throughout their educational journey.

Creating a schedule that satisfies the needs of all classrooms is a challenge that can rarely be met, but we worked very hard to develop one that approached this essential goal. For most of my tenure at TPS, each student had eight 50-minute periods each week devoted to what we called "specials"—art, music, Spanish,[4] and physical education—and one period of all-unit chorus. As a result, students were out of their unit classrooms two periods on four days; on the fifth day, children attended chorus before boarding the school bus to the nature center or a city destination. One period each day was devoted to teacher planning or a team meeting, and a second period allowed, for example, in kindergarten, each teacher to work with one-half or one-fourth of the class when two teachers were available. In other words, this schedule made it possible for a teacher to work with as few as 6 to 12 students for one full period each day.

Despite being located in rented space in a commercial structure originally built to house a pie-baking factory, we were able to design classrooms and situate them to be maximally conducive to creating a community of learners, responding to changing programmatic needs, and meeting the developmental needs of students. As school enrollment grew, we took over more and more space, eventually purchasing the building in 1990.

Remodeling always took into consideration ease of collaboration and connectedness. By design, students of each unit walked past other units to get to music, art, Spanish, chorus, and physical education. Specialist classrooms were spread throughout the school as much as possible so they were rightly perceived as fully integrated into the educational program.[5] Classrooms

---

4. Spanish eventually became a full academic subject in Middle School, meeting four periods each week. Fifth graders also increased Spanish study to three times a week.

5. Spanish classes all ended up in an area called Patagonia, which included a large open area and three individual classrooms. This was meant to be temporary, but unfortunately during my tenure classes continued in this space because of space constraints.

were designed to accommodate different developmental needs and were flexible so that with changing needs for the program, the space could be altered. We took advantage of the renovations to the middle school in 2000 to enhance its relationship to the rest of the school; for example, a fish tank was installed at its entrance to attract the younger students down the hall to pass by and engage with the middle schoolers.

We always prioritized classroom spaces. We chose not to have a central library; each classroom had its own library with a generous supply of books, both fiction and nonfiction, providing easy access for students to select books for reading and for research. The teachers chose the books for the classroom library to match the student needs and interests, as well as the changing thematic units. By eliminating the need for a full-time librarian, we were able to provide an ever-growing supply of books. (The cost of replacing a few misplaced books was also far less than a librarian's salary.)

PRESCHOOL

Our youngest learners, aged three and four, needed the reassurance of a connection between home and school. The preschool schedule included an hour-long morning drop-off period, giving teachers the time to greet parents (and other caregivers) and children individually in the classroom each day. Pick-up was also in the classroom at the end of the day. Preschoolers not only had a rich thematic classroom experience but also had 20-minute Spanish, art, and music classes in the preschool space, as well as physical education classes in the school's gym. By its second year of operation, the preschool fully occupied the third floor of the building. There was a dedicated art teacher and art room in the preschool space. The third-floor location was not ideal, with our youngest students climbing three flights of stairs no fewer than two times a day. When a city-owned property a block away became available for sale in 2005, we immediately planned to bid on it to create a new home for the preschool.

PRIMARY UNIT (KINDERGARTEN)

For most of my time at The Philadelphia School, kindergarten was the main enrollment point for students. Ready to say good-bye to their caregivers in the schoolyard, they climbed the stairs to their second-floor classroom. The space and schedule afforded time for play and exploration, as well as small-group activities. Half of the class remained in the classroom while the other half left the classroom for twice-weekly art, music, Spanish, and physical education classes. The two classroom teachers then divided the half class in two, creating very small groups for literacy and math activities. This was also a good time for large, long-term project work, for example, creating the world of Michelangelo by having the children lie on their backs and paint murals on paper attached to the underside of tables! The classroom also had a separate room for block building; the children were able to build huge structures that could remain standing, creating opportunities for collaborative imaginary play for days on end. Oftentimes a "time machine" stood at the entrance to the classroom—the children passed through and imagined that they were entering an exciting world of wonder.

PRIMARY UNIT (GRADES 1–2)

The Primary Unit classrooms were located next to and, later, across from each other.[6] Their proximity allowed for easy teacher and student collaboration between classes. Activity time was at the same time in each classroom, and teachers from one classroom sometimes visited the others as "read-aloud guests." In this way, students became known to all the Primary Unit teachers, not just their own.

The Primary Unit schedule was designed to facilitate opportunities for flexible groupings in reading and mathematics instruction.

6. Throughout this book I will be describing classrooms as they were for most of my time as principal. Since enrollment continued to grow each year, we added classrooms and team members.

Language Arts. Each day, half of the class at a time went to specials. Of the approximately twenty-four students assigned to a team of two teachers, a group of twelve would go to a special. (In addition, once a day the entire class went to specials at the same time, allowing for a planning period each day for the team.) The team of two teachers divided the twelve remaining students into two groups by achievement level (as measured on a reading inventory and by teacher observation) for instruction. Each teacher had two groups, one each period when the class was divided in half. In this way, we could accommodate four reading levels, usually ranging from beginning readers to fourth grade.

Mathematics. Math was taught at a common time for all three Primary Unit classrooms, which allowed teachers to provide six levels of instruction, with some children leaving their classroom to work with a group in another classroom. Decades later, one alumnus proudly remembered that in the course of an entire school year, he only once forgot to go to the other classroom!

JUNIOR UNIT (GRADES 3–5)

As mentioned earlier, after many years as a vertically integrated group of third, fourth, and fifth graders, the teachers recommended that third grade become a stand-alone grade in order for the children to consolidate skills. Depending on enrollment, there was one third grade classroom with a teaching team of two or three; the room consisted of three open yet separate learning spaces.

In developing their program, fourth and fifth grade teachers were sensitive to the particular needs of nine- and ten-year-old children. They recognized what developmental psychologist Erik Erikson described as an identity crisis to be resolved: industry vs. inferiority.[7] When children of this age are placed in an intermediate or a low academic group, they can feel demoralized. By emphasizing that we all develop at different rates in dif-

7. E.H. Erikson, *Childhood and Society* (New York: W.W. Norton, 1958).

ferent areas, we were able to group homogeneously. We pointed out that some could pitch a baseball, sing on key, and read complex material yet at the same time needed to work harder on mastering other skills.

The teachers experimented with various approaches to minimize negative effects of homogeneous grouping. They came up with solutions that gave students an active role in determining their quarterly placement in language arts and mathematics class (theme and science were heterogeneously grouped). Because the students understood what their own needs were, most were invested in the group that they joined or worked especially hard to move up to the next group in the next quarter. This carefully crafted approach was only possible because of the teachers' creativity, willingness to oversee a relatively complicated process, and dedication to providing each child what they needed to succeed.

Language Arts/Reading. All fourth and fifth grade teachers were available at the same time for language arts instruction. Students were originally grouped homogeneously by the teachers. After experimenting with a few alternatives, the teachers decided to try student-selected, "guided choice" groups of 14 students each. The teachers introduced five different theme-related books, each one varying in level of difficulty (4th–7th grade). To help choose among the books, the students used the "five-finger test," literally counting on their fingers the numbers of words they did not understand on a page of each book. If they knew all the words on the page, they might deem the book too easy; if they didn't understand five words or more, it was too difficult. Each student listed a first, second, and third choice.[8] If a student's first choice was deemed not appropriate, too easy or too challenging, the

---

8. Teachers made it clear to the students that they did not know which book they would be teaching because they didn't want the choice to be the teacher instead of the book. They also encouraged the students not to base their choice on that of their friends.

child's advisor met with the student to discuss the choice. If the book was too easy, the child was strongly encouraged to select a more challenging book and usually did so. If the book was too difficult and the child insisted, perhaps because the story was of particular interest, the teacher would call the parents and ask them to read the text along with the child at home. We found that a mistake made was not repeated in the next cycle; students self-corrected their next book choice and joined a more appropriate book group.

This individualized approach was more complicated than assigning a reading group based on a literacy screen. But it addressed multiple goals: to counter any stigma related to placement, to give students choice, to enable children to recognize where they were in their own learning, and to motivate students to take responsibility for their learning.

Mathematics. Over the years, Junior Unit teachers tried out several approaches to math instruction. A process similar to that in language arts, with the same goals, guided math placement. All five math classes met at the same time. At the start of the school year, the students took a five-page basic arithmetic screen, with each page increasing in difficulty. After reviewing the results with their advisors, they placed themselves, with advisor guidance, in the math group that they felt met their needs. Most children placed themselves in the appropriate group. If students requested to be placed in a more demanding math group, we allowed them to try. Our goal was to help them be realistic about what they needed and how hard they had to work. The groups were somewhat flexible so if a student made extraordinary progress, we allowed that child to move to a more advanced group.

Workshop. A special feature of Junior Unit was twice-a-week Workshop. While half the class was out in specials, the remaining students worked independently on a variety of assignments, including silent reading, catching up on past work, and theme projects.[9] During workshop teachers worked with individuals on reading or with a small group to review number facts relating to the four operations with whole numbers. This was also the time when a child who perhaps wished to move up to the next math group worked with the teacher of that group to learn the material. Workshop was an opportunity to give support or enrichment to those who needed it. It was key to the success of the guided choice approach to grouping, and yet another way teachers met the individual needs of their children.

MIDDLE SCHOOL (GRADES 6–8)

In 1989 the Carnegie Corporation of New York, a major force in educational reform, published *Turning Points: Preparing American Youth for the 21st Century*. The report called on educators to make schools smaller, more flexible, and more conducive to close relationships between students and adults. In its discussion of middle school, recommendations included assigning every student an advisor; allowing small groups of students to work on projects, thus building on adolescent preoccupation with social relationships; organizing teachers into interdisciplinary teams with discretion to modify curriculum, schedules, and other aspects of learning to meet changing student needs; encouraging community service and peer tutoring; and overall providing intense intellectual stimulation. These recommendations were inconsistent with the then-common belief that cognitive development is on hold during adolescence.

Turning Points affirmed our approach to educating our preadolescents and adolescents. Teaching middle schoolers requires understanding their needs and certainly not subscribing fully to what is popularly cited as Aristotle's jaundiced characterization: "Teenagers these days are out of control. They eat like pigs, they

9. "Best of all was the freedom we were given. We had a class called workshop [in the Junior Unit], in which we actually were able to choose what we wanted to do." (Milena Velis '97)

are disrespectful of adults, they interrupt and contradict their parents and they terrorize their teachers."

Yes, adolescents can be disrespectful, do interrupt, do contradict, and make a mess when they eat. But middle school students can also be model citizens who are thoughtful, reasonable, and cooperative. These conflicting characteristics can appear within minutes of each other.

Space considerations. The Middle School consisted of a large central area surrounded by several open classrooms. The classrooms had noise-reducing partitions but no doors, which created a sense of togetherness even when classes were in session. Between class periods, students crossed paths in the central area and had an opportunity to chat, providing the additional moments for socialization needed by adolescents throughout the day.

Bonding with advisors. Each of our middle school teachers was not only a specialist in one or two academic disciplines but also played an important role in students' social-emotional well-being. Each student had an advisor—the same advisor—for all three years of middle school. Teachers, because they are not the student's parents, often become an adolescent's confidants and role models. The relationship with an advisor can become one of a middle schooler's most important relationships, sometimes even above "best friend."

A relationship of caring and trust developed through weekly journal entries written by the student to the advisor and to which the advisor responded. Many journal entries were about everyday events (sports, a television show, a book), but more often students wrote about dreams and aspirations, as well as concerns and issues that they were reluctant to share with peers. Students expressed fears arising from conflict with family values, sibling rivalry, peer conflicts, self-worth, sexuality, adoption, fitting in, and just about every human emotion connected to their experiences. A journal entry might read like this one: "Lately my family has been struggling. . . . I have been feeling very depressed and have been watching my little brother. . . . I feel it interferes with my schoolwork and I don't know what is more important, my family or my schoolwork."

In response, the advisor would write back with suggestions but, more importantly, would keep a watchful eye on the student. There was implicit confidentiality in the journaling, but in a situation where an advisor felt a child was contemplating risky behavior or self-harm, they would contact the school psychologist and talk to the parents. The small sampling of journal entries below demonstrates how journaling is a powerful tool to help develop a trusting and caring relationship between student and advisor.

One advisor, a prolific journal responder, sometimes wrote in poetic form. A response, perhaps for a student struggling with anxiety, went like this:

> The strange thing
> About my bed
> Is that nightly
> I rejoice
> To snuggle there,
> And find bed
> The best place ever.
> Yet almost every morning I rejoice to leave.

The following journal exchange was memorable enough that the student featured it in her graduation speech.

September 2001

Dear Virginia,

I sort of have mixed feelings about school this year. I am excited about school starting, but I am not very good at change . . . as in changing my advisor. You are extremely nice and I am glad it is you who is my new advisor. Love always, Julia

Dear Julia,

I see a lot of people often resist and fight change to the point where they end up missing out on some of the pleasant surprises that come with it! Virginia

June 2002

Dear Virginia,

It has been such a long year! So much has happened and changed since sixth grade. Love always, Julia

Dear Julia,

The thing that I really admire about you, Julia, is that you have worked through your problems and "taken the higher road"—i.e., not being insensitive and selfish. I am proud of what you have accomplished this year. I am so lucky to have worked with such a talented and welcoming advisee. I still read your first entry to me and smile. Your words were so reassuring, and I knew at that moment that I had a good, supportive crew of advisees to help me through my first year. Virginia

Teachers learning alongside students. Our middle school teachers were specialists in one or more of five disciplines: language arts, thematic studies, science, mathematics, or Spanish. They loved learning, whether in their area of expertise or wherever questions or related topics led them. They collaborated on projects regardless of their academic field; the math and science teachers directed Shakespeare plays, for example. New themes excited the teachers, challenged them, and did not intimidate them. In fact, they preferred to design new curricula rather than repeat, year after the year, the same material. They were role models for lifelong learning and its importance in building community. Their own inquisitiveness enabled them to design lessons not from the viewpoint of an expert but that of a new learner, understanding that the beginner needed a connection to past experience, time, and repetition before mastery.[10]

Grouping and scheduling. Class size remained a constant consideration, and flexible grouping, based on content and student needs, was a feature of the program. Science and theme were taught in mixed-grade groups of sixth, seventh, and eighth graders. Half of the middle school was in theme class, while the other half was in science. Those halves were taught as a whole group or subdivided into halves or thirds (the desired student teacher ratio was 15 to 1). Teachers taught language arts, math, and Spanish in graded groups. Again, taking advantage of reduced class size when some of the students were in specials, the remaining students were divided for language arts, math, and Spanish by grade, usually divided into halves or thirds depending on class size.

Students were grouped homogenously for math and somewhat homogenously for language arts. In language arts, students read different versions of the same book or books of varying difficulty related to the theme. The grammar book was leveled as well. Eighth graders studied Latin in heterogeneous groups. In math, our aim was to master arithmetic and, for those who were ready for abstraction, to complete the first year of algebra by graduation.[11] Because of the wide variations in time for development of the part of the brain needed for abstraction, some eighth graders were not ready for algebra. Despite this, most of the inde-

10. "I will always remember you saying to learn something new, as it is humbling to remember what it feels like to be a student. I think it is so important never to lose sight of what it feels like to be a student—learning things for the first time—very, very humbling!" (Mary Beth Fedirko, preschool teacher)

11. The class of 1993 included a group of students who finished Algebra 1 in 7th grade. The following year they studied a variety of topics in mathematics rather than moving on to geometry. If they had completed geometry before entering high school, their math needs (Algebra 2) would have been out of sync with the rest of their high school's 9th grade schedule.

pendent high schools in the area required completion of Algebra 1 for acceptance, and we felt pressure to meet this requirement. We were conflicted about that goal, and it was a topic of ongoing discussion and review.

Project work. Middle school students are ready for long-term, complicated projects. They are ready not only to grapple with complex content but also to learn how to structure their time. Our middle schoolers wrote a formal research report each year at the completion of the thematic study, and there were also long-term science projects. Students selected their topics to match their interests and learning style. They presented their work to their classmates and parents, as well as to children and teachers from other units. Over the course of their three years in the middle school, they could see for themselves their growth as students—they recognized their journey from the concrete to the conceptual.

Friday checkout. The middle school teachers created a spread-sheet that captured each student's weekly performance in every class, including specials. During checkout period, on Friday afternoon, each student met with their advisor to see if there was any unfinished work due. If there was, the child worked on it during the checkout period and then handed it in. If the student owed too much work to finish in one period, they stayed after school, under the supervision of a teacher, for as long as it took to complete it. For most students, staying late once, while watching friends head off to socialize after school, was enough to encourage them to be more responsible about staying on top of their work. There was no stigma attached to staying late; peers commiserated with their friends.

CHAPTER 7

In Their Own Words

In order to teach you, I must know you.
Lisa Delpit, Ed.D., MacArthur "Genius" Fellow
for research on school-community relations
and cross-cultural communication

IN THE PREVIOUS CHAPTER, I wrote about how we built connections between teachers and students. The primary goal was to make sure each and every child felt known and valued. Eighth grade graduation speeches were filled with expressions of appreciation, love, and respect toward the teachers. While most tended to focus on their most recent teachers in the middle school, many were tributes to teachers in earlier grades. Here are a few excerpts.

David: "And for the past nine years, on February 6, I have come to expect a birthday treat awaiting me in my cubby. Anne [my kindergarten teacher] has never forgotten that we share a birthday. She also knows that no matter how big I get, a little gift will remind me of how important she is to me, and I am to her."

Molly: "Chris is the person who has taught me, helped me, and coached me for the past three years. He has been my surrogate parent as well as the best teacher of all time. Yes, Chris is my middle school science teacher and my advisor, but he is also much much more than that. . . ."

Anna: "Susan was my first and second grade teacher. I entered Primary Unit B as a small, scared little girl whose goals were set high though her head hung low. Susan's talent first showed as she read my journals, which had two vowels per entry, if she was lucky. Deciphering those hidden messages, she found a special way into my heart, which at the time was drowning in a sea of pain and pressure because of my parents' divorce. I remember one day when I walked into school having just had an extremely hard morning. Susan saw the stress on my face and wrapping her arms around my body, she allowed me to empty my soul onto her shoulder and that was not the only time that she was there for me. Susan has been there for me countless times, even after I left her comfortable classroom and moved on to the Junior Unit and the Middle School."

James: "When I entered sixth grade, I wasn't yet a fully formed individual; you could find me at the edge of the group, and I didn't talk too often. Then I met Steve . . . Steve has shown me that if a task must be done, it is more rewarding to do it well. Now I am better about doing and taking pride in my work. Steve helped me to build my confidence. Because of Steve, I can show everyone who I really am."

Sara: "I don't know what I am going to do next year, Judith, I know that no teacher I ever meet in the future will be able to fill the spot that you, Tom, Leish, Neesa, Art Jeff, Maria, Michael, Dan, Janet, Tricia, Miriam, and Anne have in my heart. Anne first noticed and sparked my interest in art; Janet and Tricia taught me to read, what a great gift. Miriam helped me find my voice as a writer. And, Judith, those personal journals, which inspire us to step away from our busy day, slow down, and try to understand and appreciate this life we have, I will miss writing and sharing with you."

Caitlin: "I had heard about the legend, Emily, Middle School Theme Teacher, fire-breathing dragon, with an annual appetite for theme reports . . . I soon realized that she would never live up to her reputation. As a teacher, she was inspiring and demanded only the best from everyone. As an advisor, she always had good solutions for whatever problem—social or academic. I would say that this dragon has become one of my most treasured friends. I can talk to her about anything, and I've never opened up to anyone the same way I have with her. I hope all the dragons I encounter in the future turn out to be just like Emily."

Jake: "Over the past years I have been able to develop great relationships with all of my teachers. One of these relationships was with my Junior Unit advisor, Michael. This man has a love for teaching that I have never seen before coming to TPS. In fourth grade we were learning about NASA, and we had planned to watch the movie Apollo 13. To see the movie, we had to move all the tables out of Michael's room and move 60 chairs into his room. We were ready to see the movie and Michael would briefly summarize what we were about to see and why it would be so interesting—5 minutes . . . 10 minutes . . . 20 minutes . . . 40 minutes. The period was over, chairs and tables replaced, and we had not seen any of the movie. I loved it. It took about eight weeks to finish the movie, but that is not the point. Michael had the ability to make me not care about the movie. The fact that he had so much fun teaching made everything fun to learn. When Michael teaches, he combines seriousness, interest, humor, and fun. He is not only an amazing teacher but a great friend and companion. If I had trouble with anything, I knew that I could go to him for help, and I would get it. He's a person that wants to share his knowledge with others . . . just because."

Leah: "I have learned so much from Chris, from science to a cappella, getting his jokes to getting the classroom job I wanted, and realizing that hard work really does pay off in many different ways. He has been both a teacher and a friend, and I am so glad that I have had Chris as my advisor."

Cara [writing about two of her teachers, both named Anne]: Anne G. took the whole kindergarten class on a field trip to her house to meet the famous Bics.[1] After a tour of her house, we had a picnic at a nearby park, and she bought us all treats from the ice cream truck. Anne C., my Junior Unit advisor, actually invited her nine fifth grade advisees to her house for dinner and a sleepover! Who would be brave enough to do that? Both of these teachers had a huge impact on my life. By making our relationships so personal, they taught me that a teacher can be a friend as well as an instructor."

Ivana: "I just realized that Emily and I have written more than 100 [journal] entries to each other. I have gotten to know Emily through all of our formal correspondence. Every week I looked forward to her response."

Lily: "Laura, my advisor, was really fun and easy to talk to. I could write to Laura about anything. Whenever I needed someone to talk to, I wrote to Laura about what was bothering me, and she helped . . . whatever I wrote about, Laura was always listening."

Mike: "In the beginning of the year, I was shy about my Spanish, and I didn't raise my hand too often in class. Lisa told me not to give up, to slow done. Now I can write two-page essays in Spanish, and when I went to Mexico, I spoke Spanish even when we didn't need to."

Stephen: "There are few people in the world who make you happy at the sight of them. . . . I have been very lucky to meet one such person here at The Philadelphia School, a man named Michael. I have always liked to learn, but it was Michael who taught me to love it. . . . Michael had the ability to make everything I did with him interesting. From leaping onto a table in math class wielding a meter stick to demonstrate frac-

1. Anne Greenwald had a collection of Bic lighters, all different colors and designs. She would introduce them, a unique one, with a back story and personality, at the classroom birthday celebration of each of the children in her kindergarten. Anne was loved by each child and family, and she loved each child, always finding something unique and wonderful about each one.

tions to sending us on a space mission, his genius for teaching was never exhausted."

To be sure, we didn't need to wait for Graduation Day to learn how much a teacher meant to a student. Below, a Primary Unit parent expressed appreciation for the connection between her son and teacher Barbara Stanley:

> In observing you in the classroom this year, we have been consistently impressed with your ability to individualize instruction in a way that makes every child with whom you interact feel special. Daniel's interest in reading, his ability to express himself in writing, and his enthusiasm for publicly displaying these skills are clearly attributable to your establishing with him a personal connection that nurtured his motivation to succeed. Daniel clearly sees you as one of the most important persons in his world, and he is enormously pleased that you will be his teacher for another year.

Our teachers gave so much of themselves to their students. This generosity, matched by their professionalism as educators and kindness as human beings, clearly made a huge impression on the children they taught.

CHAPTER 8

Building Student Connections

Human relationships are the essential ingredient that
catalyzes healthy development and learning.
Linda Darling-Hammond,
education professor emerita,
Stanford University

IN AN EDUCATIONAL SETTING, a strong community with the shared values of respect, responsibility, and care cannot be formed from the top down. The children need to feel connected to each other, not only in their own classroom but across the school. Although divided into units, we thought of ourselves as one school, one student body, one community. Some of the ways we nurtured student connections are described below.

FAMILY GROUPS

In the fall, each middle school student (grades 6–8) became a "family group leader," assigned three or four younger students to work with and mentor throughout the school year. For example, an eighth grader might lead a family group consisting of a fifth grader, a third grader, a second grader, and a kindergartener. A faculty member was assigned to guide the group. Family groups met several times a year for various activities, oftentimes related to the all-school theme. They sat together at assemblies and spent time once or twice a year engaged in activities out at our

74

country campus. The younger children felt very connected to their older family group members, and they were excited to see them in the hall, at the playground, or at an all-school activity. One eighth grader, Max, summed up the experience this way:

> The object of family groups is to impart a sense of caring for other members in your family, or community. For example, family groups shared their special spots at Shelly Ridge where they wrote in journals and observed nature. Sometimes, however, the idea of responsibility to others in your group didn't always get through, like when the younger members of my group tried to trade me in for someone else. . . . Nevertheless, the idea that everybody in the community should care for one another was reinforced.

TIME TOGETHER AT OUR COUNTRY CAMPUS

Spending one day a week outdoors in the fall and spring gave children the opportunity to connect to each other in new ways in a beautiful open space. Whenever possible at our outdoor facility, we tried to have all units study the same topic concurrently, with increasing complexity suited to students' ages. In this way, all students—even our youngest learners—shared a common pursuit and could have meaningful conversations with each other and take part in related activities together.

STUDENT COUNCIL

Student Council consisted of middle school officers and representatives from every unit except preschool and kindergarten. Election for officers was school-wide. Each candidate hung campaign posters around the school, introduced themselves to students in the schoolyard, and gave speeches to the student body. Their campaigns were honest, polite, and fair. Promises to install candy machines or provide longer recess were not permitted. As much as we prepared students to lose, it was still a painful lesson in democracy, as expressed by Mollie:

I didn't think of myself as someone who tries to win everything—it sort of came naturally. But this year, I ran for Student Council president, and by some miscalculation, I lost. But TPS by then had taught me that winning wasn't everything. It was a win/win situation. For instance, I got my Monday recesses back. I'd just like to thank TPS for teaching me this valuable life lesson.

Student Council representatives were chosen in each classroom. The selection was done in an age-appropriate way. For example, in the Primary Unit, all first and second graders who expressed an interest in being a class representative gave speeches; afterwards their names were placed in a container, and the name pulled out became the representative. Each child who ran had the opportunity to attend a Student Council meeting with the "elected" representative.

Student Council meetings, supervised by a faculty or staff member, were notable for the respect shown by our oldest students to the youngest members, who often had some of the best ideas. Student Council ran bake sales and food drives to raise money for causes that they deemed important; organized all-school events, such as the Annual Talent Show; and attempted to solve such problems as determining which areas of Markward Playground were to be used by which students during recess (for example, the play equipment, the basketball court, or the field).

STUDENT VS. TEACHER GAMES

After the close of each middle school athletic season, the students and teachers would compete against each other. Each fall, we headed to the field at Markward Playground, located a few blocks from the school, for an exciting soccer game. Upon completion of our full-sized gymnasium in 2001, student-versus-faculty volleyball and basketball games were added. Cheered on by the entire student body, the middle school team—win or lose—was a unifying force for our children.

SPECIAL ALL-SCHOOL EVENTS

In the 15+ years since I left The Philadelphia School, there has been controversy regarding the celebration of what may have once been religious holidays but are now American traditions. As a nonsectarian school, we did celebrate Halloween with a costumed parade and assembly, and we shared a Thanksgiving Feast of vegetarian lasagna and other foods prepared by the children in class the day before. Another community-building special event for students and staff was the annual Talent Show.

Halloween. Many of us remember Halloween as being one of the most fun-filled times of our childhood. Today some schools have banned Halloween, renamed it (for example, Autumn Festival), or given it a banal or adult-selected theme ("let's all wear funny hats").[1] For me, Halloween is a day when children can assume any animate or inanimate role that they like—but mostly fantasy characters who are beautiful, funny, or a bit frightening. I believe Halloween is a healthy opportunity for children to feel they have some control over the dark side that they know exists. They play with these ideas and feel powerful, a feeling that young children rarely experience. They play with the dark forces and know they can survive.

On Halloween, the office staff wended their way throughout the school and, playing Orff instruments, picked up the children and teachers in each classroom and led them to the multipurpose room or, in later years, the gym for an assembly. Teaching teams and office staff wore costumes, often thematic (lots of trees during the "Forest" theme, for example), and sat among the children. Besides being fun, Halloween was an opportunity

---

1. A number of schools across the U.S. have decided to end Halloween costumes and celebrations in an effort to be more inclusive to other students—those whose families do not celebrate Halloween for religious reasons or who find purchasing a costume a hardship. I know that many non-Christian families viewed Halloween as one of the few holidays that is not sectarian but "American."

for categorizing, a skill emphasized throughout our curricula. It was also an opportunity for individual decision-making, asking students to balance choice of costume with responsibility to the community. It was a rare occasion to have to ask a student to not participate.

From a small platform in the front of the room, I asked the students to listen carefully and decide which category their "character" belonged to; for example, "Are you found in the sky?" "Underground?" "In the kitchen?" "In a book?" "In a film?" As I announced each category, children had to decide if that was the one they belonged in. Each child had their moment to shine when they came to the front of the assembly and announced, over a microphone, who or what they were. For example, if the category was things that fly, ghosts, birds, fairies, bats, and a broom might approach the microphone. (I loved the broom, hoping that the child was associating it with having listened to the "Sorcerer's Apprentice" from *Fantasia* in music class!) If the occasional child stepped up and announced that they were, say, a flower in a seemingly unrelated category, no one would contradict their category decision. The decision might have been made out of fear that they might not have a chance at the microphone or because they simply had not quite grasped the meaning of the category. Some children were a bit shy, so their family group leader or sibling would accompany them to the microphone.

Thanksgiving Feast. On the day before Thanksgiving break, the entire school shared a feast prepared by the students. Earlier in the week, each unit made something to share with the entire school: the kindergarteners made "baby butters" by jumping up and down and shaking cream in small jars; Primary Unit made cornbread or salad; Junior Unit baked brownies; and Middle School took on the major project of making vegetarian lasagnas. Parent volunteers picked the lasagnas up to bake and return to school the next morning in time for the feast. Place cards were made by students in art class, and the after-school program designed centerpieces related to the all-school theme. The multipurpose room and, later, the gymnasium were filled with tables, each seating two family groups, one or two faculty or staff members, and a special guest from the wider TPS community—perhaps a bus driver or a member of the cleaning crew.

Naturally, the Thanksgiving Feast was all about being thankful—and eating delicious food. I usually opened the feast with a short historical lesson, perhaps about Lincoln declaring the First Thanksgiving. One year I gave a short talk in Spanish, hoping the eighth graders would translate for the assembled. I am not sure if I was the problem or my translators, but the audience looked completely baffled. This was a failed experiment not to be repeated, yet it represented the intellectual risks I encouraged even in the face of failure. Failure is okay, and I did not mind being a model for that philosophy. (Admittedly, since all the children studied Spanish—middle schoolers four times a week and younger students twice a week—I had hoped for a better result!)

Before the meal was served, a few classrooms sang a song, recited poetry, or spoke about something for which they were grateful. Afterwards, the middle schoolers served lunch to their family group members and invited guests. They were responsible for the younger children, often encouraging them to at least taste the lasagna before moving on to the brownies. After everyone was dismissed back to their classrooms, the eighth grade remained to clean up the room and help organize the leftovers for delivery to a nearby shelter for Philadelphians experiencing homelessness.

The Thanksgiving Feast captured the essence of what a community ought to be—individuals working together to serve not only the members of its own community but also communities that are in need of their help.

Talent Show. Organized and emceed by the Student Council, usually on or close to Valentine's Day, the Talent Show was a highly anticipated annual event. With an audience limited to students and staff, the show was meant to be pure fun. Students in kindergarten through eighth grade applied as individual or group performers, auditioned (mainly so the Student Council could record their names and the props, musical instruments, or accompaniment needed),[2] and on the day of the show wowed the audience with a variety of talents. There were skits, gymnastics, songs, jokes, ball throwing, piano playing, dancing, jump roping, and more. Student Council members comforted any children who expressed fear when it was their turn to perform. Regardless of the level of talent displayed, the student audience was appreciative and supportive. The show did seem endless— it lasted at least through two periods—with about 20 percent of the student body taking part! But it was well worth it. It gave children as young as five or six years old the opportunity to express themselves in front of a large audience, and it was a celebration of a community that supported each other.

2. In very rare instances a child would not "pass" the audition, primarily because they came totally unprepared and were clearly not making a serious effort.

CHAPTER 9

Connecting with Families

Oh, The Philadelphia School—the Buddhist school, right?
Anonymous Philadelphian

IT GOES WITHOUT SAYING that a successful school needs the support and engagement of parents and guardians, the individuals who have critically important perspectives on their children's relationships, interests, and experiences outside the school. This information enhances a teacher's understanding of a child and contributes to more effective teaching. To earn this support, a school must prioritize a family's understanding—without buzzwords, hyperbole, or equivocation—of the school's mission, program, and practice.

The Philadelphia School looked and often sounded different from most families' own educational experience—no desks in a row, mixed-age grouping, children working together at tables or reading cross-legged on the floor, teachers called by their first name—and to many parents and guardians of prospective students, this seemed, at first glance, odd and unstructured. The effort to earn trust began the moment the family of a prospective student crossed the school threshold. In the admissions process, it was critical that parents and guardians were treated with respect, honesty, and openness.

Our success in growing enrollment at The Philadelphia School largely depended on an admissions director who was fully committed to our program and a faculty who were excited to share their work with prospective families. I tried to meet with every parent or guardian who took one of our small-group admission tours, which were scheduled during the school day three or occasionally four times a week in the fall and early winter. Before I move on to discuss how we kept enrolled families well informed of our educational program—why we did the things we did (often referred to by TPS families as the "TPS way")—and their children's progress, I will digress here to share in some detail our admissions process.

Admissions Process

Before we opened our preschool in 2000, new enrollment each year consisted of a full kindergarten class, a handful of spots in first grade, and a few openings in grades 2–7. Most applicant families were from the school's immediate and surrounding neighborhoods. They learned about the school mostly by word of mouth, though our admissions staff participated in various school fairs and neighborhood festivals. Economic diversity was achievable to a large degree. Our tuition was lower than that of other independent schools, and tuition assistance was available (in 2006, 25% of the student body received financial assistance of varying amounts). I believed strongly that the children of faculty and staff should benefit from the education they provided for other children, and tuition assistance and free afterschool care were made available to them.

We strived to achieve greater racial diversity, but we did not meet our goals, especially among Black and Latino students. We respected the reasons families of color did not apply to or choose our school; many of them were shared by the white families who decided to send their children elsewhere. We were a young school, certainly compared to the other independent schools in the Philadelphia region, and some parents felt that they wanted a school with a centuries-old track record. Some were uncomfortable with the untraditional program and classroom set-up and with what they perceived as a too casual relationship between students and teachers.

As the area around the school grew more and more gentrified in the late 1990s and 2000s, our recruitment efforts needed to reach underrepresented communities living well beyond the neighborhood of the school, and transportation issues (long SEPTA or School District bus rides) were a drawback. Finally, many Black families did not want to enroll their children in a majority white school, where they might be the only Black students in a classroom. The problem of under-representation persists in most area independent schools, particularly relating to the enrollment of Black students.

Early in my tenure as principal, because of financial constraints, diversity efforts were focused in the middle school. Many families of color needed significant tuition assistance, and we had funds to provide aid for only two or three years. We ultimately realized that since our educational program was designed as a full K–8 experience, we were shortchanging the children who entered the school as middle schoolers. As our enrollment and budget grew, we focused much of our diversity efforts on recruitment for kindergarten and, later, preschool.

We held an evening Admissions Open House in the fall. Because the building's exterior had the feel of its original industrial days, it was important that prospective families tour the interior. The hallway walls adorned with student work, the spacious classrooms, the well-equipped art rooms, and the music rooms filled with every conceivable instrument belied the building's commercial origins. Equally important was meeting our faculty—all were expected to be in attendance—and learning, directly from them, about our educational program. To assist in communicating the school's distinctive character, a teacher from each unit volunteered to speak to our guests in a meeting before the tour of the building. To model the depth and thematic approach that characterized our program, teachers all focused on one selected topic. One year that topic was journal writing, a subject that demonstrated both the close bonds between students and their teachers and the continuity in building skills from kindergarten through eighth grade.

These writings showed the gradual mastery of skills:

Kindergarten journal entry: I ROTE A SENTNZ

First grade journal entry: BEN FRANKLIN FLW A KIT

Junior Unit entry: Christopher Columbus was a good navigator, but he did lots of bad things.

Eighth grade journal entry: Dear Judith, It seems to me sometimes that I don't know how I'll deal with leaving TPS. . . . I can't comprehend how to describe you or your amazing impact on your students—those "beloved scholars." Judith, these personal journals, which inspire us to step away from our busy day, slow down, and try to understand and appreciate this life we have, were so important for me. I've only been doing these journals [with you] for three years and yet I'll miss them so much. So, good life, dear Judith, and Judith, what's it all about anyway?

After the teachers' presentations, attendees toured the classrooms and had an opportunity to speak with the teachers. We encouraged our guests to plan to take part in a day-time small-group tour; seeing the school in the evening, without children, is no substitute for experiencing the vibrancy of an actual school day.

For many years, our admissions office consisted of only an admissions director, who conducted tours several times a week. The tours ended with an informal meeting—not an interview— with me and the admissions director in my office. This informational session was an opportunity for questions or comments about what had been seen on the tour; it was a learning experience for me, as applicant families spoke to one another about their school search experiences.[1] Afterwards, we spoke sepa-

---

1. These meetings were occasionally unintentional "intelligence-gathering" opportunities, with families discussing in my presence their thoughts about other schools they were considering for their children!

rately with anyone who had individual concerns or questions, often about financial aid. We met with many wonderful people, most often from the surrounding neighborhood of the school. Whether or not they planned to apply to the school, we enjoyed meeting them and recognized the value in acquainting them personally with our program.[2]

After applying for kindergarten admission, the children attended a Saturday playday.[3] The purpose was to observe the applicants in a school-like setting to evaluate their readiness for kindergarten. The children engaged in free play, listened and responded to a story, took part in a group music activity, and were evaluated for language and math readiness. While the children were in the classroom, their families had the opportunity to meet with me and the parent of a current student and ask questions. We ended each playday with a song about colors in which the children, teachers, and parents participated. The goal, aside from evaluation, was for everyone to leave with good feelings, having spent a playful morning.

How can you really evaluate a three- or four-year-old in a few hours on a Saturday morning? They are all beautiful, joyous, and remarkable little people. What teachers were looking for were any obvious language or math difficulties that might be a result of age or cognitive challenges, as well as for readiness to participate in group activities. We wanted to be sure that we could meet the needs of each child we accepted. Although we preferred that children entering kindergarten be five years of age by the summer preceding kindergarten, we did evaluate younger children for readiness. The rate of development can vary with each individual, and therefore we did not have an arbitrary cut-off.

Acceptance, which was need-blind, was limited by the num-

2. In my last year at TPS, 2005–2006, 145 tours were conducted (each tour consisting of the parents or guardians of 3 or 4 children), followed by 212 applications.

3. The preschool had its own admissions process, and applicants for grades 1–7 spent two days at TPS (in their then-current grade).

ber of openings and the expected yield rate, i.e., the number of accepted children who would actually enroll. This rate was based on an average of the previous few years. (One year we were completely wrong, and every child we accepted, accepted us. We gave the parents the option of withdrawing given that the class would be larger than expected. No one dropped out, and we hired a third classroom teacher to keep the student-teacher ratio at 12:1.)

In putting a kindergarten class together, we aimed to balance the number of girls and boys and to aim for a class that was diverse socioeconomically, racially, and ethnically.[4] One kindergarten teacher opined that the class should always include "a pair of twins and a child with glasses"! It was rare that we outright rejected an applicant, but rather we placed children on a waiting list. When there was a rejection, we would discuss the reason with the parents if they asked for an explanation. As the school became better known, resulting in many more applications, it pained us to be unable to accept more of the children. But we were committed to a small student-teacher ratio and to our current location, and we unfortunately could not accommodate all the families interested in enrolling their children in our school.

Preschool admission was run separately by the preschool director. The process followed many of the same procedures, including playdays to observe the children. In the early years of our preschool, we had a small class of three-year-olds and two classes of four-year-olds. Evaluating children for readiness at this age was very challenging. Acceptance in the preschool class did not guarantee admission to the K–8 program, although these

---

4. Except for a handful of children, our students were Philadelphians. Living in downtown Philadelphia was more affordable then than it is today. Because of this, we were able to achieve a student body of greater socioeconomic diversity. (Teachers and staff who lived closest to the school had the "privilege" of responding to the occasional "mis-setting" of the alarm system in the evening!)

children had priority unless we believed that the program did not meet that child's needs.

Enrolled Families

It was important that families continued to be well informed throughout their children's journey from preschool through eighth grade. The scope and sequence of our program did not always align with that of area school districts and more traditional independent schools. It was not uncommon for our families to learn that a child at another school was, for example, learning long division earlier than a TPS student. We reassured families by explaining the reasoning for our curricular decisions, mostly based on age-appropriateness.

We provided numerous pathways for families to be well-informed and engaged members of the school community. Each new family was assigned a welcoming family—an already enrolled family whose child was about the same age as the new student; many of these families arranged to meet before the first day of school. We held a new family orientation on the morning of the first day of school. Back-to-School Nights, which took place in the first few weeks of school, were opportunities for parents and guardians to meet the classroom and specialist teachers and learn about the year's curriculum.

PARENTS ASSOCIATION

The Philadelphia School Association (TPSA) held monthly evening meetings at which upcoming events were planned and past events reviewed. I attended TPSA meetings, as did the director of admissions and the director of development. Many events and other initiatives would have been impossible without the active participation of TPSA, for example, Grandparents and Special Friends Day, the Book Fair, and the End-of-Year Picnic. I believe that my team's active partnership with TPSA translated into a parent body that better understood and trusted the mission, values, and needs of the school.

COFFEE WITH THE PRINCIPAL

Each month I hosted an informal morning get-together in my office. The parents brought their coffee, and the school provided pastries. There was no agenda, beyond my being available to address concerns or interests a parent or guardian happened to have. I like to think that families appreciated my availability and responsiveness to their questions. Common topics were homework, the outdoor program, and testing. A recurrent issue brought up by parents who spoke Spanish at home was the desire for an accelerated Spanish program for their children. Today's technology, unavailable at the time, could provide the acceleration requested, but—besides some differentiation during class—we were unable to create additional class sections for these students.[5] These meetings gave parents an opportunity to be heard and helped us clear up concerns.

WEEKLY REMINDERS

Each week parents received a short communication that included reminders about upcoming school events. The note also thanked by name any parent who had volunteered in some capacity for the school in the previous week. Pre-Internet, this was a paper document that was sent home in the children's lunchboxes ("lunchbox express") and often found a home behind a refrigerator magnet.

CLASSROOM NOTES

Each unit sent home a weekly Friday note that described in detail the past week's classroom activities—what they were and why they were important. The note also included reminders about upcoming events specific to a particular unit or classroom. Kindergarten and Primary Unit notes regularly reminded parents to

---

5. Although we treated parents' concerns seriously, we admittedly did sometimes light-heartedly refer among ourselves to this recurrent topic as the "Spanish Inquisition." We did not approach criticism with defensiveness but with openness and good humor.

dress their children appropriately for their day in the country—long sleeves, pants, and boots!

CURRICULUM NIGHT

As in most schools, we hosted an evening, a few weeks after the start of the school year, when teachers presented to parents the year's curriculum and classroom routines and expectations. Often the parents participated in hands-on-activities in order to understand through experience what a TPS education was about. The evening initially included a presentation by specialists, but we later devoted an evening to the specialists alone; during Specialists Night, parents participated in the same physical education, art, music, and Spanish activities that their children were doing in their own classes. The following note from a parent reflects the success of Specialist Night:

> I have experienced many events and felt all kinds of emotions over my many years as a TPS parent. However, I have *never* had as much fun as I did last night. I cannot think of a better way to share pe, art, music and Spanish than to do what our kids do. It's much better than a panel discussion. Thank you!

THEME CELEBRATIONS, DRAMA AND MUSICAL PERFORMANCES, SCIENCE FAIRS, SPECIAL EVENTS

Parents and other family members had many opportunities throughout each school year to celebrate their children's learning. These not only showcased student learning but also demonstrated our program's practices in action, helping parents more fully understand our pedagogical approaches. Twice a year, Primary Unit families were invited to classroom theme celebrations, where the children proudly took them on a tour of all the rich theme-related activities they had pursued in the previous several months—writing, artwork, maps, surveys, charts, and more. A chorus performance of related songs usually preceded the classroom visit. It was impossible to leave a theme celebration without recognizing the richness of the academic program and the children's engagement in their learning. There were similar opportunities in the Junior Unit and Middle School for families not only to celebrate their child's learning but also to better understand why, for example, the arts are important avenues for internalizing content and concepts.

CONFERENCES

Twice a year, in the fall and spring, parents and guardians met with classroom teachers to discuss their children's progress academically and socially. In vertically grouped units, a family had a two- or three-year relationship with their child's teachers, resulting in a longer, collaborative view of a child's progress. We insisted that divorced parents attend conferences together so that both parents heard the same message. Our main concern was the welfare of the child. Often the student was invited to attend. I would attend some conferences to help with a complex issue or to discuss standardized test scores. I liked to attend the final conference of graduating eighth graders, and occasionally I would drop in just to share good news.

PROGRESS REPORTS

Teachers wrote narrative progress reports twice a year, in the winter and at the end of the school year. Hand-written until the prevalence of computers, the reports were highly individualized, describing in detail a child's progress. They did not compare a child's performance to that of classmates but related to parents the progress of their child's learning. If there were any concerns on the part of the teachers, remedies were offered. I asked to see any reports that mentioned particularly troubling concerns before they were mailed to families.[6] It was important to con-

---

6. All student reports were reviewed by me and by the directors of admissions and development, both of whom had writing and editing experience and knew the school well. We mostly looked for typos, but we occasionally found a "Catherine" who was called "Katherine" in a report!

firm that parents were already informed in person or by phone of these concerns before they were included in the report.

GUEST "EXPERTS"

Many of our students' families were valuable learning resources. Guest experts included, to name a few, professors of every ilk, actors, scientists, musicians, architects, artists, restaurateurs, and journalists. These guests greatly enhanced classroom studies, while at the same time gaining for themselves a fuller understanding of the school's program.

GRANDPARENTS & SPECIAL FRIENDS DAY

Each fall, grandparents and special adult friends were invited to spend several hours with their grandchild in grades K–2. Dozens of parents helped organize this busy day. TPS staff arranged a schedule so our guests (and parent volunteers) would become acquainted with our approach to teaching and learning, as well as take part in hands-on activities with the children in their classrooms. Before "attending classes," our guests, coffee and pastries in hand, met with me for a brief introduction to what they were going to see and what they wouldn't see. I picked an aspect of the program to highlight. For example, I explained why we encouraged invented spelling in our Primary Unit writing program, or why we chose a particular all-school theme, such as the *Odyssey*, and how it was made accessible to our younger students.

In the spirit of "It takes a village to raise a child," I wanted grandparents and the other adults in the children's lives to be able to ask their "host-grandchildren" specific questions about their learning. By spending time in our classrooms—taking part in theme, writing, Spanish, art, math, science or music activities—they experienced first-hand the "TPS way" and we were able to earn their support.

ANNUAL MEETING

We were required by the by-laws of our nonprofit corporation to report to the members of the Corporation (current parents and board members) about the state of the school and to elect members of the Board of Trustees for the following year. We held our Annual Meeting in May; faculty and staff were required to attend.

Rather than a dry reporting and election, we turned this into an event of appreciation—of faculty and staff, the board, and the parents. Each chair of a board committee reported on their committee's progress; for example, in 2006 the Building Committee chair reported on the recent bid on a large city-owned property at 25th and South streets, a block away from our school building.

Once the board reports were concluded, I read aloud my Annual Report to describe and honor the achievements of the faculty and staff. My report grew from a handful of pages to more than 20 pages over the course of my tenure as head of school. I read excerpts from the longer reports, but all families received the entire reports. These increasingly detailed reports reflected the robust nature of our program and the creative and thoughtful work of our teachers and staff. (They were invaluable resources for me in preparing the manuscript for this book.)

After reading the report, I presented a slideshow of photos that I and other faculty members had taken throughout the school year. The slideshow was tongue-in-cheek. To illustrate the creativity of our faculty, one slide showed a preschool teacher painting a mural completely brown. (Of course, she was preparing the background for a mural to which the children would add their colorful artwork.) Showing a photo of a teacher drinking a mock cocktail while chaperoning the eighth grade's trip to Mexico was my way of showing appreciation of the Spanish teachers' dedication to their students. Sometimes I used slides of famous works of art to comment on the school year. Munch's "The Scream" satirized the calm reactions of the faculty to student foibles, and Rousseau's "Tiger Peeking Out from the Grass" contrasted with the natural environment experienced by our students at our outdoor classroom. The faculty especially seemed to enjoy this approach, kind of a "back-door" appreciation of all they had done throughout the year.

My slideshow was followed by a song about me—usually humorous and irreverent—performed by the faculty and staff. Reflecting back to the electrical fire that broke out in the Multipurpose Room just prior to the opening of the school year, they wrote 13-verse lyrics (to the tune of "A Telegram and Ballad," from Benjamin Britten and W.H. Auden) and regaled the meeting attendees. Here are the first few verses.

A telegram
A telegram from the faculty
Sandy Dean is the name
Is the name of the addressee.
A cold wind blew thru the Northwest wood
Sandy and Mike come if you could
A fire has leveled day care and beyond
The harpsicord, piano—we need a magic wand.
Call fire-Dex and its happy crew
They cleaned all the chairs and ceiling too
They went over every cranny and nook
But damaged goods were not the only thing they took.
Into our midst our savior came,
Mechanics is the talent McGuire's the name
Can you find it, can you fix it, can you make it disappear
We need 500 chairs and the parents are all here.

For me, the Annual Meeting encapsulated—and communicated—the essence of TPS, blending serious discourse, humor, community, and appreciation.

ENGAGING FAMILIES in the life of the school was key to our success in retaining our students from preschool through eighth grade. I will never forget how our school community came together on the tragic day of September 11, 2001. Parents seemed to just show up—not to make sure their own kids were okay but to grab a Rolodex and start calling families to arrange for an emergency early dismissal. We were a family. Parents, teachers, and staff taking care of our children and each other.

CHAPTER 10

The City

Beyond the School Walls

> *Cities have the capability of providing something*
> *for everybody, only because, and only when,*
> *they are created by everybody.*
>
> Jane Jacobs

TRUE TO OUR MOTTO "City Country Classroom," we made the most of Philadelphia's historical, educational, cultural, and civic resources. The city was a natural extension of the classroom. In the winter months, especially, when students were not heading out to our country classroom, teachers planned trips to city venues to complement their classroom studies. In the course of their time at The Philadelphia School, students had many opportunities each year to get to know Philadelphia and engage in the life of the city. Whether they remained Philadelphia residents as adults in the future or not, as students they learned that cities are complex systems whose functioning depends on their citizens' understanding of past, present, and future social, economic, and environmental challenges.

The Philadelphia School is located within walking distance of the University of Pennsylvania, Drexel University, and the University of the Arts. The Rosenbach Museum & Library (now known as The Rosenbach) is a 10-minute walk away. A short bus ride away are a cornucopia of cultural resources, including the Parkway Central Library, the Philadelphia Zoo, Independence Mall, Fairmount Park, the Philadelphia Museum of Art, the Barnes Foundation, Mother Bethel AME Church, Reading Terminal, the Academy of Music, the Kimmel Center for the Performing Arts, the Franklin Institute, and the Academy of Natural Sciences.

Over the years the faculty and staff developed strong, long-term relationships with several of these organizations and institutions. The Penn Museum of Archaeology and Anthropology was the monthly destination for our middle schoolers during their study of ancient cultures. Similarly, the Philadelphia Museum of Art's galleries served as middle school classrooms for their medieval curriculum. The Rosenbach staff involved our students on various projects derived from their vast collection of some of the best-known literary and historical objects in the world. The universities were a source of professional development opportunities for teachers and staff.

Whenever possible, we sought mutually beneficial relationships with local institutions. Our faculty mentored student teachers from several area colleges and universities. For several years our Primary Unit classrooms were part of Penn Science, a science-teaching program led by Ryda Rose, an education professor at the University of Pennsylvania.

A faculty member served on the board of the Friends of Schuylkill River Park. This riverside park—with its playground, playing fields, and tennis and basketball courts—was an invaluable neighborhood amenity that our students used daily for recess and sports. We supported the park by contributing to fund-raising efforts and taking part in the annual fall festival. We often made our building available at no cost for community use; for example, our gymnasium was used by the Taney Baseball League for registration and coach training. TPS was a stop on the Center City Residents' Association's House Tour for several years, and we hosted the association's Halloween party for children. We were happy to publicize and take part in community and city-wide events. While our many field trips to venues around the city complemented our curriculum, an additional goal was to foster the next generation of city denizens, audiences, and museum-goers.

The value of meeting people with real-world experience in the topics a child is studying cannot be overestimated. Philadelphians, many of them TPS parents, made up the majority of our guest speakers—authors, journalists, professors, scientists, politicians, judges, nonprofit leaders, museum educators, social workers, city planners, artists, and musicians. Renowned urban planner Edmund Bacon took part in an all-school symposium called "Working with the City," and Franklin Institute chief astronomer Derek Pitts participated in a symposium called "Working with Science." Mayor (and later Governor) Ed Rendell shot baskets with a few of our middle schoolers at the groundbreaking of our new gymnasium (he was also one of our graduation speakers), and players from the Philadelphia Eagles rolled up their sleeves and assisted a group of students who each Monday made sandwiches after school for My Brother's House, a men's shelter about a mile from TPS.

Using our city's resources so authentically and regularly also helped our young school become well known. Children dressed in red TPS t-shirts were our best marketers as they pursued their studies outside the school building. A woman who was visiting the Barnes Foundation when our students were there took the time to write me a letter complimenting our teachers for how well prepared the children had been for their museum visit. Many of our nonparent classroom guest speakers had never even heard of the school before they entered the building; they left impressed by our teachers, our students, and our program.

Except for a handful of children, our students were Philadelphians. Most of our teachers lived in the city as well. This certainly gave heightened meaning and authenticity to our school's engagement in the city's rich historical and cultural life.

CHAPTER 11

Connecting with the Natural World
Awe and Responsibility

One touch of nature makes the whole world kin.
William Shakespeare, *Troilus and Cressida*

PROTECTING THE ENVIRONMENT and promoting citizenship are joined by the same principle of protecting the common good. Now more than ever, as we encounter increasing climate change, we need future leaders who understand how precious and fragile our natural world is. The fundamental goal of our outdoor educational program was to empower children to develop a sense of awe for the natural world. We hoped that as adults they might become active stewards of the environment.

The Philadelphia School was at the forefront of environmental education. It had a country campus from its very beginnings in 1972. One day each week in the fall and the spring, students and faculty traveled by bus to Sycamore Farm in Ambler, a 20-acre working farm with woods, a stream, fields for games, a pond, and a three-story barn.[1] Ponies, goats, and wild geese

1. Having read in the *Sunday Bulletin* in May 1971 about how the proposed school hoped to buy a farm outside of the city, Chris and Madge Donner generously offered to have the school use Sycamore Farm, their property in Ambler, as part of its educational program. Chris, a long-time educator, had recently retired from his position as counselor at Wissahickon High School, and he and his wife were looking forward to having schoolchildren in their lives again.

shared the space. There were occasional winter visits to Sycamore Farm, and the barn was the perfect place to enjoy hot chocolate on a cold day. In 1988, we moved our nature program to
Shelly Ridge, a Girl Scout property in the Roxborough section
of Philadelphia.[2] We lost the informality of Sycamore Farm,
but we benefited from a shorter bus ride and a wilder, more
varied landscape with hills, creeks, a quarry, and lots of little
shelters.

While regular experience in the natural world instills a sense
of responsibility for taking care of the environment, it is also a
key component of science education. By beginning their "scientific career" studying what they know—animals, rocks, soil,
weather, trees—children develop the confidence to grapple with
the more abstract scientific concepts they will encounter later in
their education. In addition, the outdoors is the perfect laboratory to apply classroom learning; for example, our middle school
science program used Shelly Ridge as a laboratory to apply classroom learning in biology, chemistry, and geology.[3] Whenever
possible, we tried to have units study the same topic concurrently, with increasing complexity suited to students' ages. In
this way, even the youngest kindergartener had something "scientific" to share with their older schoolmates.

A day at our country campus was not only devoted to science
lessons.[4] The outdoors offers children "freedom from an indoor

2. The Donner family sold the farm in 1986. Though we stayed on for
two years with the new owners, we knew we needed to find a property that
had long-term possibilities.

3. Our environmental education program received national recognition
during the 1989–90 school year, when science teacher Chris Taranta was
awarded a Christa McAuliffe Fellowship to write and disseminate our environment education curriculum.

4. Shelly Ridge was also an inspiring setting for work in disciplines
other than science—for example, journal writing, sketching, read-alouds,
haiku writing, and archaeological "digs."

world bound by order, neatness, propriety."[5] It was important for our city children, who were closely monitored much of the time whether in school or home, to have the time and space to play games, to wander amid the trees with friends, and to sit quietly and reflect. Teachers observed from a distance (a distance appropriate, of course, for each age group) and gave the children opportunities to work out relationships, to negotiate, to compromise, or to manage the occasional "you can't play with us." Of course, they stepped in if disagreements were too difficult for the children to manage.

There was plenty of time between lessons for free play. "Fort" building was a favorite activity among our youngest students (and many of the older ones). The children spent their free time building forts from natural materials found on the ground. The forts were occasionally elaborate constructions, but more often they were simply a pile of collected fallen branches. Regardless of their construction, they were magical places for the young architects. There were elaborate rules about how to enter, how to exit, who was eligible to belong, and what constituted a reason to be excluded or banished. The forts were the center of their fantasy world and the impetus for working out relationships and managing conflict. In between lessons, Middle School and Junior Unit students played games or—within whistle distance—explored the peaceful setting.

Once or twice a year, the entire school went out to our country campus and, in family groups, took part in a variety of science-based activities, as well as recreational games and quiet ambles through the woods and fields. We divided up into two teams (including teachers and staff) and played games that were quite competitive. Yet once back in the school building, students expected that when the winner of the games was announced over the PA system, it would be declared a tie. The children, for

5. Will Nix, "Nature Shapes Childhood," *Amicus*, Summer 1997, p. 33.

the most part, laughed. This is not to say that on other occasions we did not have winners and losers.

Visiting the same country campus throughout their elementary school years made an enormous impact on our students, as expressed in numerous graduation speeches, as seen below.

Zoe: "Those days outside taught me more than a day at a desk ever could. It was like a classroom without walls. There is so much beauty in nature that it's nice to experience it in a way that really lets you be part of it. Not just a nature walk, but really learning a place and going there week after week."

Matt: "For nine years I have been lucky enough to go to a school where the agenda for the week includes a day out in the woods. Science has always been one of my favorite classes."

Katie: "Creek walks were for me the highlight of school. . . . [I]t meant that you were old enough to hold your own against the forces of nature, be it branches scratching against your arms or the water seeping through your boots and getting your socks soaked for the rest of the day."

Zach: "Shelly Ridge was a place to stop and smell the roses. Somehow, at the same time, we came away understanding binomial nomenclature, capillary action, and cross pollination."

Aaron: "After one or two organized periods, it was time to eat lunch. My friends and I headed out to eat in our wondrous fort. Well, all it really was, was a tree with no leaves and a few branches. On the ground was a log to assist in climbing. It was very hard eating lunch in a tree, but it was fun. And we thought it was the coolest place on earth."

Jennifer: "Shelly Ridge provided us with a way to study systematically the science of the environment. We've had the opportunity to learn and experience it first-hand instead of just reading about it in a textbook. . . . We must not forget that city and country, people and nature, are interconnected and depend on each other for survival."

Mac: "Sycamore Farm was a big open field and a patch of woods. I loved building forts and going into the barn to warm up in the winter, huddling near the stove and drinking hot chocolate."

It was also gratifying to hear from parents, sometimes long after their children had graduated.

> What a great concept . . . imagine city kids spending a day per week in the country—when all other kids are stuck behind a desk somewhere. It may have seemed radical in 1972—but it makes as much sense today as it did then.
> —Leigh and Jean Mason (alumni parents)

CHAPTER 12

All-School Theme
A Community of Learners

The mind is not a vessel to be filled, but a fire to be kindled.

Plutarch

THEMATIC INSTRUCTION integrates basic disciplines, such as reading, mathematics, and history, within the exploration of a broad subject. It is based on the idea that knowledge is acquired best when learned in the context of a coherent "whole" and when students can connect what they are learning to the real world. A thematic approach replicates the complexity and interconnectedness of the world around us. It requires that teachers of different disciplines work together to design curriculum around a selected broad topic or concept.

At The Philadelphia School we had both an annual all-school theme and unit (or classroom) themes. Each year the students awaited the traditional "unveiling" of the all-school theme by the teachers and staff with excited anticipation. This alone fostered an investment by the entire school community in whatever theme was to be studied.

Selection of the all-school theme was a serious endeavor. Each spring, on an in-service day, the faculty gathered together to select the theme for the following year. In this way, teachers had the summer to prepare. It was a tense competition. Teachers came to the meeting prepared to lobby for a topic they were passionate about. After a rather byzantine system of voting, we narrowed the topics down to a handful of possibilities. Suggested themes had to answer most of the following questions with a "yes."

- Can the content be adapted to be appropriate for the stage of development and interest of the various age levels?
- Does the theme provide opportunities to teach new skills and to apply newly acquired skills?
- Is leveled reading material, as literature and for research (both primary and secondary sources), available?
- Are there opportunities for creative and expository writing?
- Are there opportunities to integrate Spanish, music, dance, art, drama, and physical education?
- Does the theme lead outward to other topics and content, not only spiraling inward? For example, the *Wind in the Willows* theme lent itself not only to a formal study of the characters, plot, and setting; the book also engendered scientific study of the habitat and characteristics of the animals in the story. "The Great Experiment" theme led to topics that included the history of Philadelphia, fairness, justice, the free Black people living in the city, and even the steamboat that was first seen traveling on the Delaware during the Constitutional Convention.
- Is the theme significantly different from that of previous recent themes in terms of the focus on various disciplines? For example, the *Wind and the Willows* theme, which had strong science elements, might be followed the next year with a theme with greater emphasis on history, such as "City Hall." Also if the previous year's theme had required an inordinate amount of planning, such as "Circa 1492," that theme might be followed by one less demanding.
- Are there opportunities for critical thinking? Can data be collected, compared, interpreted, and classified to

form concepts? Can generalizations be made by relating concepts?

- Are there multicultural resources to facilitate attention to multiple perspectives and the experience of historically underrepresented people of color?
- Are there upcoming major celebrations in the nation or city that could be studied and that will provide rich opportunities for field trips?

Once the three "finalist" topics were determined, faculty broke up into topic groups to research and discuss whether the topic met most of the criteria. Each group did not consist only of proponents of the particular theme being examined; this gave balance to the sometimes-unbridled enthusiasm of biased group members! We reconvened after about 45 minutes or so, and each group presented their findings. Then came the final vote, resulting in a theme we believed was the most exciting and engaging for both the students and the teachers.

All-School themes gave all members of our community a common vocabulary and common experience. They also gave the faculty insight into the perspective of learners. For instance, teachers may be reading *Wind in the Willows* for the first time along with the children, or perhaps they know very little about the architecture and sculpture of Philadelphia's City Hall. The changing themes from year to year made faculty and staff visible models of life-long learning; the students saw that learning was not just for children.

Although the next year's all-school theme was selected in the spring, the faculty and staff were sworn to secrecy until they revealed it in an assembly during the first week of school. Faculty and staff created and presented some sort of "original production"—a play, a song, or game—and afterwards the students excitedly guessed (always successfully!) what the theme was. Many children tried all summer to get someone on staff to reveal the theme. One day I found myself encircled in a neighborhood swimming pool by a large group of children who said they would not let me out of the pool until I told them what the theme was for the next school year. I was able to escape, secret intact, by diving under the students and running to the changing room. (By the way, it was the last time I swam in the neighborhood pool.)

A good deal of preparation for the all-school theme took place over the summer. One of our teachers served as theme coordinator and gathered together resources from our own libraries and from the Free Library of Philadelphia. When the teachers arrived at school for their two weeks of in-service in late August and early September, a smorgasbord of reference books, nonfiction, and fiction was awaiting them. A committee then formed to develop the theme, coordinate between units, arrange for theme-related guest speakers or performers, and plan the culminating activities.

The all-school theme usually was a focus of study for the first six to eight weeks of school. The kindergarten and Primary Unit sometimes joined in later because our youngest students needed to spend the first weeks of school getting used to daily routines (sometimes, if an all-school theme was particularly engaging and exciting, it would continue throughout a good part of the year in these classrooms). At the end of the theme study, a week or so of culminating activities took place in family groups. Here is a list of the all-school themes during my time at TPS.

- Ethnic Philadelphia
- Fantasy
- The Constitution: The Great Experiment
- The Forest
- City Hall
- Inventions
- Mathematics
- Circa 1492: A Clash of Cultures
- Grahame's *The Wind in the Willows*

- William Penn and Toleration
- The Underground
- Child Times
- The Year 1972
- Time
- Summer Olympics & Australia
- Homer's *Odyssey*
- Building Philadelphia
- Poetry: Painting with Words
- Empathy: Walking in Others' Shoes
- Benjamin Franklin: One Person Can Make a Difference

As a school located in a city with a long and fascinating history, we tended to return our attention every few years to events or individuals that had a Philadelphia connection. Whatever a school's locale, it is important to investigate the history of the area using local resources. This not only serves to spark curiosity but may also motivate students to value and preserve their heritage. The next several pages are devoted to descriptions of several of our all-school themes, which demonstrate the power of interdisciplinary thematic study in terms of skill development, student and teacher engagement, and community building. Below are the general categories of the all-school themes from 1983 to 2006.

- the anniversary of a historic event
- a current event
- a work of literature
- the natural environment
- a historic site
- a concept
- a historic figure

The sampling of all-school themes below is not organized in chronological order but rather follows in the order of the topics listed above. I recommend that the reader look back to the list of theme criteria to get an idea of how each theme met them.

The Constitution: The Great Experiment
(1987–88 School Year)

Our all-school theme in 1987–88 celebrated the Bicentennial of the U. S. Constitution, written in Philadelphia in the same Independence Hall that stands on Chestnut Street today. In fact, the very chair on which George Washington sat to oversee the proceedings is still in place there, with the image of a sun etched on the back of the chair. After the Constitution was adopted, Benjamin Franklin was to have said, "I wasn't sure if we had a rising or setting sun when we began but I now believe it to be a rising sun."

Making this study appropriate for all ages in the school was a challenge, but we did just that. We were convinced that even young children could understand the value of liberty and of organizing government consistent with preserving personal freedom and civic responsibility. Children understood oppressed and oppressor. At the very least, our students would memorize information that they would come to understand in time; for example, all the children learned the Preamble of the Constitution, set to music by our music teacher, yet it might take a few years before our younger students understood it fully. At best, the children would grasp the significance of the Constitution as it related to their lives. They stepped into the shoes of the founding fathers to experience the conflicts and accomplishments of the 55 delegates, and they and their teachers enjoyed being part of the nation's 200th birthday party. A goal of this study was to tap into issues that all students understood—the issues of fairness, justice, the need for rules or laws, and freedom coupled with responsibility.

The youngest children studied Philadelphia "firsts" (for example, first hospital, first public library, first American flag) and colonial Philadelphia. The Junior Unit explored the concept of peace and the reasons why a constitution was needed. In a simulation with students representing the 13 colonies, the Junior Unit held a bake sale with each of the 13 original colonies using its own currency. Finding equivalents was a wonderful mathematics problem but frustrating if one actually wanted to buy a cookie. The need for a common currency was made real. The Middle School began its study of the Constitution with a look at democracy in ancient Greece.

The arts were central to this particular theme study. Music and drama brought the 18th century alive for children living 200 years later! Three faculty members wrote a musical, *The Great Experiment, 1787,* which dramatized the debates surrounding the writing of the document at the Constitutional Convention. The production, which received an award from the Bicentennial Leadership Project, included some of the actual language of the delegates as they struggled to compromise and write the text. The entire student body, together with some faculty and the chorus of Philadelphia Center for Older People, performed the musical at Penn's Landing in the Port of History Museum auditorium as part of the City of Philadelphia's We the People 200 celebration.

William Penn and Toleration (1994–95)

We took advantage of another city-wide celebration, the 350th birthday of William Penn, the founder of Philadelphia, to develop an all-school theme that was rich in local history and took a look at the then-radical notion of toleration, which guided Penn in his "Holy Experiment" in religious toleration in his new colony.[1] There were many local venues to visit, city-wide events to attend, and a general buzz about William Penn's birthday throughout the city during the school year.

The study of tolerance—and intolerance—was especially pertinent to our five-year-olds, who were emerging from an egocentric stage of development and struggling to accept different

1. The terms "toleration" and "tolerance" were used by Penn and his 17th-century contemporaries in the context of religious freedom. Today those words are rightly challenged and aptly replaced by "inclusion."

points of view. In fact, one might say that teaching and learning inclusion was the essential focus of the Primary Unit years; they continued their study with the examples of extreme intolerance in *Alice in Wonderland*.

Fourth and fifth graders reenacted the trial of Penn that led him to imprisonment and eventually to the New World to found Philadelphia. Third graders focused on the meaning of religious tolerance and compared religious beliefs of the present with those flourishing in the late 17th and early 18th centuries.

Middle schoolers compared Penn's vision of the city to the reality they saw touring neighborhoods with the executive director of the Foundation for Architecture. They looked at legislation, industrialization, new technologies, and the economy in light of how such developments affect the viability of Penn's vison as the ideal for the present. Middle schoolers read non-fiction to prepare for debates about creationism vs. evolution, immigration law, and gays in the military. From a socio-emotional standpoint, a focus on tolerance and intolerance was fitting for middle schoolers, who can tend to regress temporarily to a state of egocentricity, when they are subject to abrupt mood swings, rejection of authority, and extreme views. Students and teachers worked together to create a forum for their feelings about tolerance in the original musical production "Voices."

As mentioned earlier, an important criterion for an all-school theme was the availability of good literature. Among the literary works selected to address the issues of inclusion were *The Giver* and *Number the Stars* by Lois Lowry, *Trumpeter of the Swans* and *Stuart Little* by E.B. White, *The Witch of Blackbird Pond* by Elizabeth George Speare, *The One Hundred Dresses* by Eleanor Estes, and *The Curse of the Squirrel* by Laurence Yep.

A theme celebration took place at Shelly Ridge, where family groups took part in role playing to practice conflict resolution, as well as built shelters similar to what the first European settlers may have constructed in Philadelphia.

Learning that the William Penn statue atop City Hall was in need of repair, our students decided that the people of Philadelphia should save the statue. Unaware that a fund was being established for this purpose, the children decided to hold a bake sale to raise renovation money. They presented Mayor Goode with a check in a City Hall ceremony. Their presentation speeches were so admired by the mayor that the children—two students from the Primary Unit and two from the Junior Unit—were asked to speak at the unveiling of the restored William Penn statue before a crowd of hundreds at Dilworth Plaza.

Circa 1492: Clash of Cultures (1992–93)

October 1992 was the 500th anniversary of Columbus's journey to what was then considered by Europeans as the "New World." In anticipation of nation-wide attention to this anniversary, the faculty felt it was a timely and robust topic for the all-school theme. A wealth of resources, representing a variety of perspectives, would be available for the study.

As usual, the theme was a "state secret" until the always exciting first-day-of-school assembly. The entire faculty and staff presented their original play "Enterprise of the Indies," based on our summer reading *Conquest of Paradise: Christopher Columbus and the Columbian Legacy* by Kirkpatrick Sale. The faculty-written play included facts and theories about the planning and financing of the voyage of Columbus and posed questions that we hoped would motivate students to explore the topic. (As with many opening assemblies, many of our youngest students went home that first day and reported to parents that they had no idea what theme the teachers had unveiled in their performance! But that was part of the fun.)

All students investigated the concepts of differences, exploration, cooperation, cultural encounter, and change, but they learned through contexts that were developmentally appropriate. For example, Primary Unit studied Columbus's first voyage; topics of their study included weather, sailing ships, navigation, the crew, and geography. The children considered their own experiences of traveling to places that were new to them; they compared their own expectations when "finding" a beach and ocean with Columbus's expectations of finding gold and a new route to Asia. In art they drew and painted ships and murals of the Columbian voyage and Bosch-like monsters that Columbus's crew might have thought inhabited the ocean. The children wrote journal entries as they imagined traveling on one of Columbus's three ships. Rainforests were created in all Primary Unit classrooms.

Junior Unit studied Europe in 1492 to shed light on the forces that shaped Columbus. They then turned their attention to the "New World," writing a musical about the conflict between developers, Maya, environmentalists, and archaeologists. In art class they created ceramic Maya stelae and a "rainforest" set for their production. In language arts they read novels relating to Columbus or to the themes of voyage and oceans.

Middle School studied the impact of the encounter between Native Americans and Europeans. They wrote encounter stories and invented cultures as part of an archaeological project. In art class they drew botanical illustrations of the indigenous plants that Columbus might have found, and they created Aztec-Maya designs. As a culminating activity the middle schoolers shared their work with students in other units; and all students, in family groups, traveled throughout the school to see the theme-related environments created by each unit.

Spanish language was a natural connection. In Spanish classes, students read or listened to tales, myths, and legends from South and Central America. Junior Unit and Middle School students studied the geography and cultures of Spanish-speaking countries. In physical education, children played Native American games.

Toward the end of the all-school theme study, the students were asked to decide who they would have liked to have been in 1492. Most of the children understood the complexities of this question and were aware of the multiple perspectives to be considered. With the exception of several young students who stated they would have liked to have been Queen Isabella, they were unable to make a choice. (No one chose the role of a Taino because of their dreadful treatment.) The question of Columbus's hero status was unsettled, although those who had read the diaries of Las Casas believed Columbus to be a villain.

This all-school theme was an engaging and compelling avenue for learning and internalizing skills. Students read for information, wrote fiction and essays, studied geography, learned about the flora and fauna (comparing those of San Salvador and Hispaniola to those found at our country campus), listened to and played music of the 16th century, and visited the Philadelphia Museum of Art to see paintings of the period. Guest experts gave lectures to the older students, for example, about the Jews of Spain and the Conversos.

Summer Olympics & Australia (2000–01)

The opening of our new gymnasium coincided with the 2000 summer Olympics in Sydney, so it seemed fitting to open the new school year with the study of the Olympics and Australia. We knew that there would be considerable interest in the topic among our students, as well as a great deal of media focus. Our physical education teacher, who sometimes struggled to find authentic connections to the all-school theme, was delighted to finally have a theme that spotlighted sports!

To prepare, the faculty read Bill Bryson's *In a Sunburned Country*. During our in-service weeks before the opening of school, Barbara Tobin, a native of Perth and professor of children's literature at the University of Pennsylvania, taught the faculty about the geography of the continent, aspects of aboriginal culture, and Australian children's literature. To introduce the all-school theme at our opening day assembly, the faculty and staff marched around the gymnasium singing "Kookaburra" and carrying flags of countries participating in the Olympics. This time it took only a few minutes for the students to guess the theme.

The kindergarten, in conjunction with its science theme of water, focused on "underwater Australia," looking at the continent's marine life. They studied the Great Barrier Reef, home of one-third of all the earth's fish species, and studied the fish and mammal life inhabiting the waters around Australia. First and second graders learned about the history, symbolism, and traditions of the games. The various summer sports were highlighted, and they read biographies of a number of athletes, stressing the importance of practice and good sportsmanship. They worked in small groups to research and share information about a variety of animals indigenous to the continent. Australia proved to be such an engaging theme for their students that the Primary Unit teachers continued with the theme throughout the remainder of the year. The children created detailed maps of Australia and then transformed their classrooms into the Australian Outback, the Rainforest, and the Great Barrier Reef.

The third grade (at that time known as JU-B and no longer vertically grouped with the fourth and fifth grades) focused on how the Australian continent's geography determined, in part, how people met their basic needs, how people needed to cooperate to survive, how belief systems and myths developed to help people make sense of their world, and how environmental changes caused cultural change. Their study of Aboriginal Australians centered on their beliefs, stories, and artistic traditions. The students compared myths from different parts of Australia and created a Venn diagram to organize the similarities and differences between them. Literature enriching the theme included Aboriginal stories, such as *Warnayarra the Rainbow Snake*.

Fourth and fifth graders (then known as JU-A) compared the ancient and modern Olympic games; they examined cultural and political changes, such as the inclusion of women in 1900, the introduction of the Paralympics in 1960, and the joint appearance of the North and South Korean teams in the opening ceremony in the summer 2000 games. They studied the geography, demography, and physical size of Australia; learned about the Great Barrier Reef; and took a look at the cane toad and its ecological niche. Activities included dramatizing the story of the Stolen Generation, learning the Australian national anthem, and paragraph writing about Australia and comparing the ancient and modern Olympics.

Middle School students focused on geography to understand the multinational aspects of the Olympic movement. They charted the progress of Olympic athletes from around the world in their own Olympic booklet, and they each chose a specific country to study in some depth. Students read and discussed Australian literature, noting similarities and differences in language and culture. The culmination of this study took place on All-School Shelly Ridge Day. Each middle schooler taught their family group about the nation that group represented in our own "parade of nations"; family groups competed in Olympic style races and physical challenges, and they collaborated on a sponge painting inspired by Aboriginal Australian art.

Wind in the Willows (1993–94)

The *Wind in the Willows* theme was our first all-school theme based on a book. Kenneth Grahame's novel had appeal to all ages. To unveil the theme, the faculty performed an excerpt from William Perry's Broadway 1985 musical *The Wind in the Willows*. Throughout the theme study, all units explored the concepts of friendship and justice. The Primary Unit and Junior Unit studied animals, habitats, and environments. The Junior Unit re-created scenes from the book with puppets and book-in-hand theater. *Wind and the Willows* was a relaxing read-aloud for middle schoolers out in the "wilds" of Shelly Ridge. Middle schoolers worked on pastel drawings of mounted animal specimens borrowed from the Academy of Natural Sciences; the drawings, seen throughout the school, helped the book come alive. The physical education curriculum paid tribute to the theme with games such as Whack a Mole, Frog in the Bucket, and Toad Hall Casino.

The *Wind in the Willows* theme stands out as one of the most successful in terms of mixed-age project work. Two-and-a-half days of mixed-aged workshops and projects culminated in a final day of presentations and a picnic at Toad Hall (better known as the multipurpose room). For the workshops, faculty developed a wide variety of activities that pertained to the book. Students were given a choice of activities and grouped in a way that balanced age and activity preference. The activities offered were writing the further adventures of Rat, Mole, Badger, and Toad; preparing food that was mentioned in the book and eaten at Toad's picnic (and writing and illustrating a cookbook with the recipes); building a diorama of the setting, including Wild Wood, Riverbank, and Mole's house; writing music for the songs in the book; storytelling (which included performing an episode with music and puppets); English games of the period; exploring things that move (motors, trolleys, and solar-powered cars); writing for the newspaper River Bank Express; and constructing an animal alphabet book after a zoo trip to observe animals.

Homer's *Odyssey* (2001–02)

I strove to assemble a faculty that did not shy away from sophisticated content, and the success of this theme was incredibly rewarding to me. The faculty and staff read the *Odyssey* for their summer assignment. For some, this meant revisiting the epic poem; for others, it was a new experience. In-service work in late August and early September included a presentation by *Inquirer* film critic and TPS parent Carrie Rickey about odyssey themes in movies, such as *Oh, Brother! Where Art Thou?* For the first time, we brought in professionals—Tucker's Tales Puppet Theatre—to present the theme at the first school assembly. Early into the theme study several well-known Philadelphians, including Mayor John Street and restaurateur Stephen Starr, participated in a six-morning *Odyssey* read-aloud in the gymnasium. The read-aloud was kicked off by alumnus Mac Marston, who read the prologue in ancient Greek.

Age-appropriate versions of the *Odyssey* were read in each of the classrooms, from kindergarten through the Middle School. The kindergarten used the *Odyssey* as the start of a year-long study of journeys. The children drew mythological figures and constellations, and groups created models representing Odysseus and his castle, the Cyclops, Scylla and Charybdis, the Sirens, and Circe and Odysseus's men. The concept of journeys was reinforced through other literature, including Carle's *Rooster's Off to See the World*, Cleary's *The Mouse and the Motorcycle*, Dahl's *James and the Giant Peach*, and Carroll's *Alice's Adventures in Wonderland*.

The Primary Unit classrooms read several versions of the *Odyssey*. Activities included drawing a picture after each chapter was read aloud, group retellings of the story, and creating a "memory game" from the epic poem. Students discussed how actions lead to consequences, how people make choices and use skills to resolve differences, and how a story can be told from various points of view.

In Junior Unit, the story of Odysseus was enriched by a study of Greek mythology, the Trojan War, and Mediterranean geography. They created a bulletin board of Greek gods. The third graders created *Odyssey* storyboards and a Greek gods mural, focusing on the gods of Mount Olympus. Students examined how people used cunning to overcome hardship, how religion was an important part of ancient Greek culture, and how acts of hubris were often followed by punishment and misfortune (as they saw in the section about the Cyclops).

Middle School students focused on the stories and myths in which Homer's epic poem is grounded. Having a thorough knowledge of the mythology Homer used to tell his story allowed the reader to understand the story on a number of levels. How the people of Homer's time envisioned the unknown, explained the mechanisms of cause and effect, and made concrete various abstractions such as good, evil, beauty, truth, and justice—these questions informed classroom inquiry. I asked the middle schoolers to consider this question: Was Odysseus a hero or a scoundrel for abandoning his family for the sake of adventure? A lesson on mythology in art at the Philadelphia Museum of Art challenged students to identify the stories represented in the museum's collection of European paintings and sculpture. Cy Twombly's "Fifty Days at Iliam," depicting the final days of the Trojan War, was a highlight of their museum visit.

The *Odyssey* was a particularly inspiring theme for the physical education, drama, and art teachers. All of our students, from preschool through eighth grade, navigated obstacle courses inspired by the challenges faced by Odysseus and his crew. In drama classes, middle schoolers studied an abridged version of Euripides *Iphigenia in Aulis*; they wrote a scene designed to precede the actual play, prepared and presented a series of "freeze frames" representing a particularly dramatic scene, and devised staging for the final scene. Junior Unit classes dramatized the myth of Persephone. In the art room, the *Odyssey* inspired the creation of ceramic monster masks in kindergarten classes; equation paintings of mythological creatures in Primary Unit classes; and an iMovie animation representing a "virtual journey" in Middle School classes.

Shelly Ridge was the perfect site for our final sharing of project work. Students created four mythical cultures—inhabiting the quarry, the meadow, the beech forest, and the field—which students speculated that Odysseus might have encountered on his journey home to Ithaca. In cross-unit project groups, students collaborated on stories, created artifacts, and performed dances, rituals, and music expressive of their mythical culture.

To be honest, I don't think any of us knew just how much an epic poem, composed more than 2,500 years ago, would resonate with children of all ages as we entered the 21st century! It was an incredibly rewarding and exhilarating experience for our community of learners. In the words of a parent:

> Over dinner I listened to my three rumpled, post-soccer practice boys discussing the all-school theme, Homer's *Odyssey*. The 9- and 12-year-old weren't sure which chapter was the best. But the 5-year-old was certain; Scylla and Charybdis was his favorite.

The Forest
(1988–89, 1999–2000)

This all-school theme fit perfectly with environmental studies at our country classroom. It was the only theme that we repeated. The faculty and staff introduced the theme with a performance of Dr. Seuss's *The Lorax* (1988–89) and sang the title song from the musical *Into the Woods* (1999–2000). The curriculum each time included both the factual and the fictional.

The kindergarten learned about mythical beasts in the forest and, using Dr. Seuss's *The Lorax*, studied the positive and negative reasons for cutting down trees, and they studied the trees adjacent to their shelter at Shelly Ridge. The children transformed their classroom into their own "Lorax Land."

Primary Unit children learned to identify six tree species by their leaves, bark, and shape and created tree identification booklets that included leaf and bark rubbings, sketches of the tree shapes, and leaf specimens; they later shared their booklets with the Middle School students, who were doing a similar project. They each created a replica of a tree they had studied as it appeared in a particular season; after these trees were "planted" in the classroom, parents were invited for "Coffee in the Forest." After reading forest-related fairy tales—"Hansel and Gretel," "Snow White and the Seven Dwarves," "Rapunzel," and "Rumpelstiltskin"—they created a retrieval chart to record and organize the characteristics of fairy tales and then generalized about the similarities and differences between characters (mean, greedy, kind, magical powers) and problem resolutions.

Junior Unit students surveyed the north slope woods at Shelly Ridge and studied the interdependence of animals, trees, and plants. Documentation of their research included descriptive and scientific writing, mapping, and artwork. A study of cycles dealt with the role of trees in the food chain. The students learned about tree anatomy and saw a demonstration of capillary action. A rap song called "The Kids as Trees" reinforced the students' understanding of the forest's ecological system. The concept of change was explored through a study of the ozone layer, photosynthesis, and the consequence of human impact on the environment. Elizabeth George Speare's *The Sign of the Beaver* was the unit's touchstone book.

Middle school students explored the question, Who Owns the Forest? They tackled the problem of the disappearance of native vegetation by building a deer exclosure at Shelly Ridge to test the hypothesis that native vegetation could survive if protected. Students also created tree identification booklets focusing on the differences between native and exotic species. Each booklet included a leaf classification chart with specimens and pressed leaves. Students in Middle School and Junior Unit worked with the Center City Greening Project to survey trees in the neighborhood, update the tree health records, and evaluate the condition of the tree pits. In addition, middle schoolers worked in Wissahickon Park to maintain trails by identifying and removing invasive vines and inserting water bars to divert water and prevent erosion.

What better way to culminate the "Forest" theme than to spend a day at Shelly Ridge! Children presented projects and plays and shared their chosen "magic spots" with their family groups.[2] A calendar produced by the Middle School featured writings about their magic spots and documented some of their feelings about the nature center. Performances of *The Wizard of Oz* and *Forestful of Music* were inspired by the forest study in 1989.

Empathy: Walking in Each Other's Shoes (2004–05)

Instead of focusing on an all-school theme for the first eight or so weeks of school, we devoted a full year's worth of attention to "Empathy." Although the concept of empathy had always been

---

2. Each child chose a specific site that they returned to each time they visited Shelly Ridge. This was a place that they felt was their very own—a place that inspired reflection, writing, and drawing.

threaded through all we did, we decided to focus on the topic as a school community. We felt that greater familiarity with the concept would benefit the children socially and as students of literature, history, and other disciplines. Empathy certainly is critical in a democracy.

The theme was kicked off by storyteller Linda Goss, who gave a dramatic reading of her book *The Frog Who Wanted to Be a Singer*. The frog is frustrated because he wants to be a singer, but no one thinks that a frog can sing. He is finally given a chance to sing, and he proves to everyone that though his singing might be different, it is quite good. His new kind of vocal style is the birth of rhythm and blues and boogie-woogie singing!

Our "Empathy" study was a literature-rich topic. Monthly all-school readings of picture books devoted to such issues as learning differences and racial prejudice were springboards for family-group and classroom discussions and activities. Family groups came together for read-alouds of the picture books *The Story of Ruby Bridges* by Robert Coles, *Crow Boy* by Taro Yashima, *Thank you, Mr. Falker* and *Mrs. Katz and Tush* by Patricia Polacco, *Miz Berlin Walks* by Jane Yolen, and *Wilfrid Gordon McDonald Partridge* by Mem Fox.

The themes in these beautifully illustrated and sensitively written picture books are universal, appropriate for most ages though older students are rarely exposed to them. The first book we read aloud, *Crow Boy*, was about a boy in Japan who was autistic, though never identified as such, and who was teased by his classmates for many years before a teacher was able to intervene to find a talent the boy could express.

Following the reading, a teacher asked, "Why do kids tease, in general?"

Student #1: "People feel threatened because the characters are different or maybe they are trying to impress their friends."

Teacher: "What could you do about It?"

Student # 2: "It depends on your size; you should get a teacher."

Student # 3: "Sometimes if you help someone who's being teased, you get teased too. Sometimes it backfires when you try to help someone."

Student #4: "Maybe you could go up to the person teasing and try to make friends with them. Or walk away. That's good because sometimes the teaser is trying to get a reaction."

Student #5: "I think teasing is serious. It really disrupts the way you feel about yourself. If someone is saying mean things you start to believe them and feel really bad about yourself. The effect can last a long time."

During this study we overheard children use the word "empathy" and watched them practice empathy as they went about their daily lives at school. Faculty members recorded student comments and responses to the readers' questions and looked for evidence of identification with the rejected individual and any attempts to understand both the victim and the bully. Responses from the first session varied from insightful comments to visceral responses. It was interesting to note that the students aged 8 to 10 felt that the victim had some responsibility to try to improve life for themselves, suggesting that they believed that each person has some control over their life. The younger children had responses that varied from "good fairy" to rather drastic action. Here are some of their comments illustrating the range of reactions:

"He'll have a growth spurt; he will come out of his shell and people will stop teasing him. He will start acting like the other boys."

"Those kids wouldn't be here because they are mean."

"Chase the mean kids cross the playground and rip their tongues out."

In a later chapter, I will talk more about how empathy, along with critical thinking, is key to education of character in a democratic society. For now, I will close this discussion with a more uplifting sentiment, expressed in a letter I received from a grandparent:

> When I picked up my grandchildren on my regular Wednesday, I asked about this year's theme. Jeremy quickly responded, "Empathy, walking in each other's shoes"; then Carolyn proceeded to elaborate on the meaning of the word. It is heartwarming to know that your staff create multiple ways for the students at TPS to embrace moral values.

Benjamin Franklin: One Person Can Make a Difference (2005–06)

"Benjamin Franklin" was the all-school theme selected by the faculty and staff for my final year at The Philadelphia School. The year was the tercentenary of Benjamin Franklin, and institutions across the city—the Kimmel Center, the Rosenbach Museum and Library, the Constitution Center, the Franklin Institute, to name a few—were featuring Franklin-related exhibits throughout the year.[3] K–8 students in every classroom also had the opportunity to visit sites frequented by Franklin himself.

Benjamin Franklin himself encapsulates thematic education, and an all-school theme devoted to him was an apt one with which to end my tenure at The Philadelphia School. Franklin was a writer, a publisher, a scientist, an inventor, a diplomat, a politician, a philosopher, a musician, and a founder of many institutions that exist to this day.

It is not hard to imagine the various ways our faculty approached this theme. Some focused on Franklin's scientific discoveries, some on his work as one of our nation's founders, and

3. Junior Unit teacher Miriam Harlan had spent part of the summer at an NEH-funded institute on teaching about Ben Franklin. She led a workshop at our summer in-service on exhibits, curricula, and other resources available to enrich our study.

others on his founding of many of Philadelphia institutions and civic organizations that our students know well, such as Pennsylvania Hospital and the University of Pennsylvania.

In addition to learning about the man himself, a study of the multi-dimensional life of this one individual was a template for any subsequent biographical examination of an individual from the past or present. And Franklin's life and work—during the founding of our country and the writing of our constitution—was a compelling entry point to understanding our nation's Great Experiment in democracy.

As much as this study of Franklin was viewed as a template for further biographical studies, it also stands out as the third theme devoted to a white man. Although most of our theme studies looked at multiple perspectives of, for example, indigenous people, enslaved Blacks, and immigrant communities, in our all-school theme selection no one ever suggested that we focus our theme on, say, W.E.B. Dubois or Octavius Catto, two of Philadelphia's early Black intellectuals, educators, and civil rights activists. Proposed theme topics did include "Jazz" and "Harlem Renaissance," but they did not receive much support among faculty.[4]

My hope is that all-school themes exemplified the richness of interdisciplinary curricula that delve deeply into a topic, encouraging children (and teachers) to examine a topic from multiple perspectives and work collaboratively on meaningful projects that foster learning.

---

4. I will address this oversight more fully in a later chapter. I will also note here that no theme ever focused on a woman or a work of literature written by a woman.

CHAPTER 13

Unit Themes
Teaching Skills Through Integrated Disciplines

*The principal goal of education is to create men and women
who are capable of doing new things, not simply repeating
what other generations have done . . . who are creative,
inventive, and discoverers, who can be critical and verify,
and not accept, everything they are offered.*

Jean Piaget

WITHIN BROAD CONSTRAINTS, each team of classroom
teachers developed their own thematic curriculum beyond the
all-school theme. This autonomy allowed teachers to pursue
their interests and to find excitement in discovery alongside
their students. Specials teachers—art, music, drama, Spanish,
and physical education—designed curricula to reinforce the
unit themes.

In the lower grades—Preschool through Primary Unit—
teachers developed their unit themes based on student and
teacher interests. It was rare for teachers to repeat a unit theme.
Topic choice was limited only by what was being taught in the
previous or next higher grade (for example, teaching the same
topic, such as "Colonial Philadelphia," one year after another
would not be optimal). The main requirement was that the
selected themes include the opportunity to work on basic reading, writing, and math skills and to express learned content in

art, music, and drama. Occasionally the unit themes touched upon topics being studied in other units, allowing for enlightening sharing opportunities.

The Primary Unit often extended the all-school theme into their unit theme. For example, after an autumn filled with the adventures of Odysseus in the *Odyssey*, the kindergarteners moved their attention away from a Mediterranean journey to *Alice's Adventures in Wonderland*. Lewis Carroll's fanciful story captured their imaginations. The children discussed how one should feel secure in being different and how one can change physically and still remain the same person. Students acted out scenes from the book, discussed how life was different when the book was written from life today, and considered what their Wonderland would be if they were Alice. By the end of the year, the children had transformed their classroom into Wonderland, complete with murals, Cheshire cats, playing cards, and cups and saucers ready for a tea party. The Keswick Theatre happened to be staging *Alice in Wonderland*, and, of course, the class boarded a school bus to see the production.

The Junior Unit designed its three-year rotation of unit themes from topics in American history. The three rotations focused on precolonial and colonial America, 19th-century America, and 20th-century America (often focusing on industry and technology). The Middle School's three-year rotation was devoted to topics related to Ancient Civilizations, the Middle Ages, and the Renaissance. Content within each rotation varied from year to year, primarily based on teacher and student interest. Each year middle schoolers wrote a theme, or research, report on a topic related to the time period but focused on any area of the world.

In the rest of this chapter, several unit themes are described in detail.

PRESCHOOL

Each year the preschool faculty created an engaging and stimulating environment for our youngest learners. In a thematic unit on the world of birds the children—in groups named the Robins, the Penguins, the Bluebirds, the Cardinals, and the Hummingbirds—learned about birds in general and then focused on the particular bird for which their group was named. During an autumn trip to Shelly Ridge the preschoolers kept their eyes peeled and their ears open to determine whether any of their feathered friends remained up north for the cold weather.

An especially ambitious and festive preschool theme was introduced after a study of how animals prepare for winter. Each preschooler took a "cruise" to escape the winter weather, traveling to Hawaii, Trinidad, Jamaica, or Puerto Rico. Before setting out, the classes read books about their destinations and engaged in project work about ships, the animals that live in the sea, and the traditional foods and music of their port of call. The culminating activity was a Calypso Carnivale, at which the children treated their families to island cuisine and entertainment.

PRIMARY UNIT

"Light the imagination!" was what long-time kindergarten teacher Anne Greenwald described as a main goal of the classroom's theme. A time machine was often stationed at the classroom's entryway, inviting the children to enter another time, past or present—to a time of dinosaurs or ancient gods and goddesses or colonial Philadelphia or the world of Michelangelo.

During the 1995–96 school year, the Primary Unit's theme was "Vikings," a topic in which geography and history played a significant role. Our first and second graders focused primarily on Scandinavian geography and its influence on a way of life, reasons for migration and emigration, and the effects of cross-cultural interaction. The kindergarten became familiar with a bit of Scandinavian geography and history. Norse myths, troll stories, and the books *Growing Up in Viking Times* and *Trouble River* are examples of literature used to teach reading and to build content and concepts related to theme. The kindergarteners studied sinking and floating (in the context of Viking ships), and first and second graders learned about icebergs, glaciers, and fjords. Specials classes were designed around the unit theme:

The children became familiar with the music of Greig's *Peer Gynt*, kindergarteners created their own versions of Munch's "The Scream," and physical education classes featured Norwegian games.

The 2005–06 all-school theme "Benjamin Franklin: One Person Can Make a Difference" was extended throughout the year in the Primary Unit. This theme was a rich interdisciplinary study that included language arts, history, geography, mathematics, and art. The children began their study by thinking about the question, "What is history?" They talked about how each one of us is part of history and how each person has a history of their own. They read and discussed three different Franklin biographies, each having a different emphasis to help students understand that history is subject to interpretation and depends on the point of view of the storyteller. Students looked at others who made a difference in American history, including Benjamin Banneker, Martin Luther King Jr., and Rosa Parks, and discussed how these heroes, through courage, love, and wisdom, changed the world around them.

The students constructed a map of the thirteen original colonies, and represented Franklin's travels between Boston and Philadelphia and across the Atlantic to London and Paris. The children looked through a variety of resources to find information about Franklin, and their research was entered on a class timeline of his life. They completed a retrieval chart of information about Franklin, wrote individual personal histories, and figured out ways to represent the number 300 (how old Ben would have been if he were alive).

With Franklin Court[1] as a model, the children decided which aspects of Franklin's life to include for their culminating theme celebration. On the day of the celebration, they and their guests were able to try out various printing techniques in the print shop

1. Franklin Court, one of the sites the children visited, consists of the archaeological remnants of Benjamin Franklin's house and nearby buildings. It was quite the experience for the children to walk in Franklin's footsteps.

they created, play a replica of a glass harmonica, and experiment with static electricity.

JUNIOR UNIT

The Junior Unit pursued a three-year American history rotation, which included study of the period prior to the arrival of European settlers. They examined the pre-colonial life of Native Americans in three regions: the Southwest, the Plains, and the Eastern Woodlands. Myths and nonfiction texts were used to help gain information about the lives and beliefs of Native Americans. Students learned how each group used the environment to meet basic needs and how there was significant diversity, along with similarities, among various Native American cultures. They then explored conflicts between the European settlers and the Native Americans.

The study of colonial America began with a look at the settlement of four early American colonies, focusing on the reasons for the founding of each colony and its geography. Students discussed the relationship between a colony and a mother country, the causes and effects of war, contradictions in the Declaration of Independence, rebellion, freedom and slavery, propaganda, and religious freedom and tolerance. Research was recorded on retrieval charts, which were used to pull together and organize the information. Students generalized based on the data and learned to base opinions on evidence. Activities crossed disciplines; for example, students wrote poems in the style of Longfellow's *Midnight Ride of Paul Revere*, wrote propaganda messages, created political cartoons about the Stamp Act, discussed Leutze's painting *Washington Crossing the Delaware*, studied battle maps, and wrote letters from the point of view of a soldier.

A culminating fourth and fifth grade project was the writing and production of the movie "Scenes from Colonial America," which was filmed on location at the 18th-century Harriton House and at Shelly Ridge. Throughout the theme study, children read historical fiction, including Ester Forbes's *Johnny Tremain*, Laurie Halse Anderson's *Fever 1793*, Julius Lester's *To Be a Slave,* Elizabeth George Speare's *The Witch of Blackbird Pond,* and several novels by James Lincoln Collier and Christopher Collier.

The focus of the third Junior Unit rotation, Industrial America, changed from time to time and included mining, sweat shops, assembly-line production, immigration, space exploration, and the westward movement. I will explore some of these studies in depth in a later chapter.

MIDDLE SCHOOL

The Middle School's three-year theme rotation was approached from a conceptual perspective. The themes were generally titled in this fashion: "From Uruk to Rome: Foundations of Western Culture," "From Chaos to Camelot: The Medieval World," and "Man as the Measure: The Renaissance World."

It was fitting that during my final year at The Philadelphia School the theme was the Middle Ages, the very topic of the Sybil Marshall workshop that introduced me early in my career to thematic, interdisciplinary study! Rather than discussing all three theme rotations, I will revisit the medieval period.

The students began this study by focusing on the collapse of the Roman Empire and on the Barbarian invasions of the fifth century CE; they participated in a simulation highlighting the challenges and the effects brought by the collapse of the Roman order. The students rotated through three project groups, each devoted to an important culture that flourished in the medieval world: Mongolia and Mali, the Vikings, and Islamic Spain.

The study of medieval communities looked at four different European models—castle, monastery, village, and town—to understand how each defined concepts central to their welfare, including community (inclusion and exclusion), power, safety, and core values. Keeping in mind that the need for power and control—and the violence that can ensue in the pursuit of fulfilling this need—is a primary issue for many adolescents, the Middle School teachers structured thematic study around issues of power and control in the Middle Ages. Children approached study of this historical period from the perspective that as many cultures flourished and vied for supremacy at this time, people slowly developed the awareness that there is a need for organizational principles that govern societies.

Field trips—including a day spent in New York City at the Cloisters—provided opportunities to learn about medieval art, architecture, warfare, and religion. Tuesdays in the winter were dedicated to the study of the First Crusade; the BBC documentary *The Crusades with Terry Jones* was a valuable resource.

Middle School students had rich literary experiences in theme and language arts classes. Works included Rosemary Sutcliff's *Dragon Slayer: The Story of Beowulf,* Robert Nye's *Beowulf: A New Telling,* R.L. Green's *King Arthur and his Knights of the Round Table,* Tennyson's "The Lady of Shalott," and A.T. Hatoo's translation of *The Nibelungenlied.*

In the spring each student wrote a research report—note cards, footnotes, bibliography, and all—on a topic of their choosing. Topics included Erasmus, the Incas, Khadijah's Influence on Muhammad, Medieval Japan, Medieval Medicine, Richard the Lionheart, The Social Role of Women in the Middle Ages, and Vlad the Impaler. The culmination of this multi-week research project was an oral presentation to classmates.

Art projects included creating illuminated letters for a bestiary, assembling a ceramic mosaic reflecting a medieval motif, and sculpting a clay gargoyle. The music curriculum featured a study of chant from the 9th through the 13th century; exploration of early forms of polyphony; and a performance of "O Fortuna," the opening movement of Karl Orff's *Carmina Burana.*

A RICH INTERDISCIPLINARY, thematic program provides the focus for learning, giving purpose and meaning to the educational experience. Students know what they are learning and why, while they are learning it. They engage in a wide variety of activities that spur curiosity, build skills, and develop an awareness of the underlying complexity of the world around them.

CHAPTER 14

The Central Role of the Arts

*It is the supreme art of the teacher to awaken joy
in creative expression and knowledge.*

Albert Einstein

*Poetry is finer and more philosophical than
history; for poetry expresses the universal,
and history only the particular.*

Aristotle

Perhaps it is music that will save the world.

Pablo Casals

I BEGIN THIS CHAPTER with three quotes rather than one to underscore how essential the arts are to an educational program.[1] The arts represent possibility—the creation of sounds, objects, stories, and movements that never existed before. This sense of possibility sparks the imagination, a key ingredient in learning and personal growth. The imagination is given license to fly. In *The Descent of Man* (1871), Charles Darwin wrote, "The imagination is one of the highest prerogatives of man. By this faculty he unites, independently of the will, former images and ideas, and thus creates brilliant and novel results."

1. I include the literary arts alongside the visual and performing arts to emphasize the importance of literature in language arts programs. No child is too young to enjoy stories and poetry—or to make some up themselves!

The arts are not add-ons or frills to be included only "if there is time" or excluded because of financial constraints or an emphasis on STEM. The intrinsic values of the arts are many for both the creator, the viewer, and the reader—they inspire creativity and innovation, stimulate thought and learning, bring people together, build empathy, develop attention to detail, spur personal and social transformation, communicate values, and express the human condition and journey. The arts enrich our lives—our experience with a piece of music, a work of art, or a poem changes who we are.

It is the artist's expression of the human experience that ultimately engages the student. And for that reason alone we teachers must find a way to bring all students along on that journey. Teaching requires artistry to exploit the power of artistry. In music class, students learn about pitch, timbre, notation, harmony, rhythm, melody, structure, and dynamics; but equally important is what musicians are expressing about their own life and times, past traditions, and their original creation. In literary studies, students learn about plot, theme, character, setting, structure, and style; but they also gain an understanding of an author's expression of the complexity and challenges of the human condition. Likewise, in the visual arts, students learn about the elements of line, light, color, and design; but they also explore artists' unique expressions of what they themselves saw as they painted.

The visual and performing arts deserve to be taught as disciplines unto themselves. But they should also be incorporated in thematic work in every classroom. At The Philadelphia School, students attended art and music (or drama) classes twice a week; all students also attended chorus class. The arts curricula were designed to relate to unit classroom thematic studies, thereby giving our students through self-expression a way of internalizing content, making meaning of experience, and making a unique statement. For example, in conjunction with a classroom study of the Maya, Junior Unit students collaborated on the creation of tall stelae characteristic of the Mesoamerican civilization; the stelae were decorated with relief sculpture that depicted scenes from Maya life. Singing a Gregorian chant or a Black spiritual helps students stand in the shoes of peoples in the past. Literature—from Christopher Paul Collier's *The Watsons Go to Birmingham* to Shakespeare's *Romeo and Juliet*—gives readers insight not only into the past but also into universal human emotions.

There is growing interest among researchers in understanding the impact of the arts on "human flourishing." In 2018, the University of Pennsylvania's Perelman School of Medicine launched the Penn Center for Neuroaesthetics, which has assembled a multidisciplinary group of researchers to investigate the nature and neural basis of beauty, art, design, and architecture. Among the questions they seek to answer is, How does engagement with aesthetics and the arts contribute to well-being? The Humanities and Human Flourishing Project, led by James O. Palewski, Principal Investigator and Project Director at Penn's Positive Psychology Center, is engaged in research into how cultural pursuits can cultivate well-being not just for individuals but for communities as well.[2] This is exciting work whose findings, I hope, will be widely disseminated in education circles.

Music

Whenever I observed a music class at The Philadelphia School, I saw expressions of joy and intense focus. And if that alone is not enough of a reason for inclusion in the curriculum, a significant number of large-scale studies have provided convincing evidence that learning music, the most abstract of the arts, enhances learning in other areas. Two Canadian studies cited in the *Wall Street Journal* in 2014 found that the effect prevails even after eliminating the influence of socio-economic status.[3]

2. For more on human flourishing, see https://jamespawelski.com/grant-for-humanities/.

3. https://www.wsj.com/articles/a-musical-fix-for-american-schools-1412954652

In the first, conducted in 2004, students were randomly assigned to keyboard lessons, lessons in singing or drama, or no lessons at all. The researchers found a significant increase in the IQ scores of the 132 first graders who studied music. In the second Canadian study, published in 2011, 48 preschoolers were found to have experienced a similar boost in IQ after only 20 days of musical training, an increase five times that of the control group.

In other research cited in the *Wall Street Journal* article, investigators found an increase, after music making, in the ability of preschoolers to organize and solve problems. In the terminology of cognitive neuroscience, those preschoolers experienced an increase in executive function. Also cited were the results of a study led by a neurobiologist at Northwestern University, who in 2013, after studying the effect of two years of musical training on 44 six- to nine-year-olds, reported a significant increase in the music students' ability to process sounds, which is key to language, reading, and focus in the classroom.

Perhaps the most striking finding was reported in a 2009 study published in the *Journal of Neuroscience* that looked at the effect of 15 months of instrumental music lessons.[4] Using MRI studies before and after the lessons, scientists discovered an increase in the size of areas of the brain that control fine motor skills and hearing, as well as in the area of the brain that connects the left and right side of the brain.

For me, equally as significant as these studies is what so many of us who have studied a musical instrument know: Playing a musical instrument builds perseverance, focus, and self-control—characteristics that research has correlated with success in school and life. Albert Einstein credited his development of the theory of relativity to "the result of musical perception."[5]

Vocal music was an important part of the curriculum. Stu-

4. https://www.jneurosci.org/content/29/10/2019

5. https://www.nytimes.com/2006/01/31/science/a-genius-finds-inspiration-in-the-music-of-another.html

dents from first through eighth grade met one period a week by unit for chorus. Standing on risers in the Multipurpose Room, students learned theme-related music to be performed in concert or as part of a unit musical or opera (often written by the students or occasionally by the faculty). Choral performances often had piano and Orff instrumental accompaniment by classmates. Primary Unit chorus performed "Invented Minds" as part of their Benjamin Franklin study, and Junior Unit students learned songs in the musical traditions of African American spirituals, work songs, blues, ragtime, and swing. The Middle School impressively learned and performed excerpts from Purcell's *Dido and Aeneas* (an opera based on Virgil's *Aeneid*) as part of their study of Ancient Civilizations and "La Fortuna" from Carl Orff's *Carmina Burana* as part of their study of the Middle Ages. Chorus was a constant throughout a child's TPS experience, leading a great many to join chorus or an a cappella group in high school and beyond.

When I retired from The Philadelphia School, one of the most meaningful tributes to my tenure at the school was the naming of one of the school's string ensembles after me. The Sandra Dean String Ensemble represents the hallmark of my efforts to establish a premier K–8 string program. Offering violin lessons to children as young as four or five enabled us to build a Primary Unit string ensemble, as well as an ensemble for the more accomplished string players. It was difficult for me to believe that I was not listening to a professional ensemble when I heard our older students perform a repertoire that included Vivaldi's Concerto for Four Violins in B minor and Concerto for Two Cellos in G minor and the chorale from Bach's Cantata No. 147. Their conductor, Aaron Picht, exuded a joyful love of music that could not help but be infectious and reflected in the children's playing and the audience's reactions. The music brought tears to my eyes not only because I was moved by such young children playing challenging pieces but also because the music itself touched on a universal truth, an almost spiritual message that seemed to speak to our better selves.

By 2006, our afterschool music program enrolled 150 children, studying voice and a wide range of instruments, including piano, guitar, strings, recorder, flute, and percussion. There were instrumental ensembles, as well as an a cappella group. The school year was punctuated by several recitals and concerts, giving our student musicians the opportunity to play for their peers and their families and building future audiences for tomorrow's music makers. None of this was possible without the extraordinary talents of our music teachers, all of whom were artists in their own right. On the occasion of my retirement, Christoph Eschenbach, music director of the Philadelphia Orchestra, wrote:

> I would like to thank TPS for helping to form future musicians and audiences. In addition to your formal music classes, you have a hugely successful after-school music program . . . and nurtured the development of an advanced chorus, an a cappella music group, and an impressive violin ensemble, as well as percussion, flute, and recorder ensembles.

Visual Arts

The studies I cited earlier found a correlation of music training and increased IQ but none or little associated with the visual arts. But I have no doubt—nor do other researchers—that access to the visual arts—as both a practitioner and a viewer—plays an important role in enhancing the learning process. The visual arts teach students to observe even the smallest details of a work of art; to envision something that does not yet exist; to find their personal voice; to think about their decisions; to persevere and work through frustration; to take risks and learn from mistakes; to develop craft; and to learn about the art world.[6] There may not be data-driven evidence about these outcomes—they are

6. L. Hetland, E. Winner, S. Veenema, and K. Sheridan, *Studio Thinking: The Real Benefits of Visual Arts Education* (New York: Teachers College Press, 2007).

unlikely to be seen on standardized tests—but as a progressive educator, I believe that the development of these habits of mind are invaluable in a democratic society.

Our art curriculum, with projects related to the all-school theme or classroom themes, gave students opportunities to express themselves through a wide variety of media while at the same time solidifying their understanding of thematic content. Middle schoolers' study of the history and culture of ancient Greece, for example, was enhanced by the creation and decoration of Greek pots in the art room. Students gained a deeper understanding of various historical periods by exploring artists' imaginative and evocative expressions of their reactions to their own surroundings and times. They left The Philadelphia School knowing the lives and work of many artists, including Leonardo DaVinci, Francisco Goya, Vincent van Gogh, Paul Cézanne, Georgia O'Keefe, Diego Rivera, Jacob Lawrence, Henri Matisse, Horace Pippin, and Mary Cassatt, as well as the work of Native American artists. Students explored how each artist viewed the world, the artistic traditions they challenged, and their unique contributions. A particularly powerful study was a comparison of the depiction of war in Pablo Picasso's "Guernica," Cy Twombly's "Fifty Days at Iliam," and Horace Pippin's World War I paintings.

The Philadelphia Museum of Art had the feel of home for our students, who visited the museum regularly during their time at TPS. Barbara Bassett, curator of education and school and teacher programs at the museum, had this to say about our art program:

> Your commitment to incorporating the visual arts into your thematic curriculum is a model that I wish more schools would adopt. . . . Your students claim the museum as an extension of their classroom. Whether it is a preschool student learning about shapes and colors, a second grader seeking inspiration for a pointillism project in art class, or a middle school student finding evi-

dence of cultural convergence during the Middle Ages, the staff of TPS have helped students to see that learning can happen anywhere.

Literary Arts

Perhaps more than music and the visual arts, literary studies—the most concrete of the arts—provide the most compelling personal expressions of the complexity of human behavior and motivation. Literature gives the reader insight into human emotions and behavior, as well as the actual language to express their own feelings. There is comfort in knowing that they are not alone, that their feelings are shared and understood by others. For example, powerlessness and issues of control are often present in the life of even the youngest child. In Maurice Sendak's *Where the Wild Things Are,* young Max manages his anger by using his imagination to create a land where he controls the environment and its inhabitants. He ultimately learns that familial love is unconditional when he finds a hot meal in his room when he "returns." The reader is comforted by the love Max receives from his family.

In Eric Rohmann's *My Friend Rabbit,* Rabbit gets into all sorts of trouble, but Mouse is a loyal, forgiving friend who understands that Rabbit means well. Young readers can relate to the idea that friends can disappoint or challenge a relationship, but that does not destroy the friendship. Children are given the language of friendship: "But Rabbit means well. And he is my friend."

So many children are shy; they do not want to stand out but want to fade into the background. In David Lucas's beautifully illustrated *Halibut Jackson,* the title character uses his imagination to do just that. But when he is invited to the birthday party of the Queen in her palace, rather than fading into the background, he uses his imagination to win the heart and esteem of the Queen. Despite his shyness, Halibut has managed to make new friends.

E.B. White's classic *Charlotte's Web* provides many examples of friendship, loyalty, and quick thinking when Charlotte saves Wilbur the pig from being butchered by weaving in her web the words "Some Pig." The reader is ultimately confronted with death when Charlotte dies but is cheered up by her offspring, who emerge yet sail away. White gives the reader the language and feeling of the journey toward independence. What parent has not cried at this moment, experiencing the beauty and the pain of separation as a child becomes independent?

We find a similar moment in Madeleine L'Engle's *Wrinkle in Time* when Meg realizes that she must go alone to save her brother—no one can make the journey or task easier or can do it for her. Meg says to her father, "I wanted you to do it all for me. I wanted everything to be all easy and simple. . . . I didn't want to have to do anything myself." "But I wanted to do it for you," Mr. Murry responded, "that's what every parent wants." Mrs. Whatsit responds, "You are a wise man, Mr. Murry. You are going to let her go." And so Meg goes alone to face the danger and save Charles Wallace. We learn we can get support and comfort from others, but we must make our own way through life.

Literature powerfully evokes empathy as a reader is introduced to new or conflicting perspectives. Harper Lee's transformational *To Kill a Mockingbird* explores the roots and consequences of racism and social injustice in an Alabama town as narrated by young Scout Finch, the daughter of a white lawyer representing a Black man wrongly accused of raping a young white woman. Homer's *Odyssey* resonates with children in terms of such themes as loyalty, perseverance, and the search for adventure, and the students can identify with Odysseus's predicament when facing the monsters Scylla and Charybdis. Where is the student who has never found themselves "between a rock and a hard place"?

The study of literature and history often intersected, and literature was incorporated whenever possible in the study of other subjects. Stories that feature children as protagonists, especially, bring history alive for young readers, helping them develop empathy and creating a sense of agency. The power of literature is transformative, as New York *Times* op-ed columnist David Brooks wrote (11/14/2021):

> A person who feeds his or her imagination with a fuller repertoire of thoughts and experiences has the ability not only to see reality more richly but also—even more rare—to imagine the world through the imaginations of others. This is the skill we see in Shakespeare to such a miraculous degree—his ability to disappear into his character and inhabit their points of view without ever pretending to explain them.

I will take a cue from David Brooks and close this section on literature with Shakespeare. The Middle School's thematic study of "Man as the Measure" focused on the cultures that flourished and interacted with each other during the period from 1400 to 1600. Students read plays by Shakespeare and, later in the year, presented a multi-play Shakespeare Festival to the school community. Dan Lai, a Junior Unit teacher and an avid theatergoer, took it upon himself to create a summary of the plays for teachers to share with our youngest students before attending the festival; while much of the dialogue was difficult for these children to understand, they loved seeing their Family Group leaders in costume wielding swords, kissing donkeys, and sprinkling fairy dust. They looked forward to performing in the plays when they became middle schoolers.

Shakespeare's plays have strong themes that continue to be relevant today—love, death, ambition, power, fate, and free will. The plays resonate with young people, helping them learn about themselves and connect with others via the comedy and drama of everyday life. The bard's contributions to the English language—his innovative craftsmanship—remain part of daily discourse. If you have ever said "in a pickle," "wild goose chase," or "it's Greek to me," you have cited Shakespeare.

Many educators are wondering if they should continue to teach Shakespeare. How much, if any, should be taught when we are committed to diversifying curricula? When considering this question, I recommend keeping Maya Angelou's words in mind: "Shakespeare—I was very influenced—still am—by Shakespeare. I couldn't believe that a white man in the 16th century could so know my heart."[7]

7. Maya Angelou, interview by Terry Gross, *Fresh Air*, NPR, 1986. For the full interview, go to https://www.npr.org/transcripts/316707321a.

CHAPTER 15

A Conceptual Approach

No matter what views people hold of the chief
function of education, they at least agree
that people need to learn to think.

Hilda Taba

A SHARED CONCEPTUAL APPROACH across grades and disciplines connects a community of learners. In every classroom, from the preschool through eighth grade, teachers should be heard asking their students, "Is there another way to solve that problem? What are the similarities and differences? Where can you find that answer? What questions do you have? What would you like to know? What is your evidence? Having students accustomed to answering such questions leads to independence and responsibility for one's own learning.

In all our classrooms, we used the work of curriculum theorist and reformer Hilda Taba (1902–1967) to teach, encourage, and reinforce thinking skills. Taba emigrated to the United States from Estonia to pursue a master's degree on the relationship of democracy and education. While working on a doctoral degree at Columbia University, she met John Dewey and other developers of the principles of progressive education. In her dissertation, she argued that education for democracy was a vital component of schooling and curricula and that it needed to be experiential, with children learning to solve problems and resolve conflicts together.

Taba believed that students generalized only after data are organized and that students could be led toward making generalizations through concept development. In the 1950s, she designed a series of strategies for teachers to use to help students develop thinking skills. Although originally designed for use in a social studies curriculum, the strategies could be applied to many disciplines, texts, or subject matters. They are a systematic way of organizing and sequencing questions to direct students' thinking and to conduct discussions according to simple rules that are equitable for all class members.

We used Taba's strategies throughout our educational program, repeating the language contained therein each year in the hope that the repetition of vocabulary and processes would have an impact on the development of the student's thinking skills. Her three major tasks, or strategies, were

- Diagnosis (listing, grouping, and labeling to form concepts)
- Interpretation and Generalization (making inferences)
- Application (predicting, forming hypotheses, verifying the prediction)

Our teachers used Taba's categories both for planning units of study and for writing final summaries of what actually occurred. Basic concepts, such as conflict and resolution, causation, interdependence, and similarities and differences, were threaded over and over again in a spiral fashion, throughout the curriculum. Planning materials and final curriculum summaries often differed because one could never completely predict where a study might go. Student interest, curiosity, and readiness, as well as the richness of material, would drive the direction of the study and the concepts involved.

Taba approached a unit of study by breaking it down into main concepts, main ideas, specific knowledge and information, academic skills, and application of knowledge. Her curricular framework served as a shared guidepost for our classroom practice.[1]

An abridged summary of the Middle School's fall 1994 study of "Tolerance" shows how teachers applied Taba's approach.

Overarching concepts:

Tolerance, differences and similarities, cultural change, creation, and adaptation.

Main ideas explored:

William Penn's goals for Philadelphia have still to be reached.
Creation and change can be studied from both a religious and a scientific perspective.
Immigration is both an opportunity and a challenge
Diversity at TPS can be examined and expressed in several ways.

Specific knowledge and information:

Centered on the ideas that (1) William Penn's ideal city was safe, comfortable, prosperous, and tolerant; (2) evolution is supported by the bulk of physical evidence, including fossil evidence, genetics, and anatomical similarities in organisms; and (3) diversity at TPS can be surveyed and analyzed.

Academic skills:

Research skills, reading primary sources (William Penn's writing), creative writing, how to use a spreadsheet and a database to sort, and how to use the public library as a resource (including experiences with InfoTrack, microfilm, catalogs, and abstracts).

Application of knowledge:

Debates (Immigration, Creationism vs Evolution, Gays in the Military), science labs, dramatic performances, and computer presentations.

1. For a more complete description of Taba's approach, see *A Teacher's Handbook to Elementary Social Studies: An Inductive Approach*, Taba, Hilda; and others (Reading, MA: Addison-Wesley, 1971).

I cannot overemphasize how influential the work of Hilda Taba was to our program. Our classroom practice reflected her fundamental belief that the selection of content does not develop the techniques and skills for thinking, change patterns of attitudes and feelings, or produce academic and social skills. These objectives only can be achieved by the way in which the learning experiences are planned and conducted in the classroom.[2]

2. Taba, 1967, p. 11.

CHAPTER 16

Teacher Autonomy

*You must trust and believe in people,
or life becomes impossible.*

Anton Chekhov

TEACHER AUTONOMY has become a major point of discussion in American public education, largely as a result of policies that limit the professionalism, authority, creativity, and effectiveness of teachers. Fundamental to my pedagogical philosophy is trusting and encouraging teachers to experiment and to follow their interests and notions of what will engage their students. Nurturing my connections to faculty and trusting them were two sides of the same coin. A high degree of teacher autonomy resulted in countless amazing and innovative programs, a few of which I will describe briefly below.

MISSION TO MARS

Michael Zimmerman, teacher and team leader of the Junior Unit, was inspired by the film *Apollo 13* to create a simulation of sending a spacecraft and an unmanned rover to Mars. Part of a year-long study of 20th-century America, the simulation was based on knowledge that the students had acquired by learning about an actual mission to Mars that NASA was planning. In preparation for their own simulated mission to the red planet, the Junior Unit also participated in activities at the Buehler Challenger and Science Center in Paramus, NJ.

Back at TPS, the students applied for jobs required for the launch. Medical technicians created and implemented a rigorous health and fitness program for the astronauts. Engineers learned about real space and weight limitations involved in the design of their trans-Martian vehicle. Robotic specialists wrote computer programs and built rovers to perform tasks on a model Martian landscape they mapped out and constructed. The astronauts cultivated oxygen- and food-producing plants; they received instruction from teammates and practiced their in-flight tasks. Flight directors learned "space speak," studied the tasks of all the other teams, and composed the mission script that coordinated all activities during the mission. Navigators learned and taught the landmarks of perpetual night; using the 12 constellations of the zodiac, they planned the path to Mars.

On the day of the mission, everyone was in position at mission control, while the astronauts were in their student-designed spacecraft. The navigators, using the trajectory they plotted, were able to show on a map the progress the shuttle made as it passed Venus on the way to Mars. During the flight, mission control created some challenges that the astronauts struggled with. It was all very real as there was some uncertainty as to whether the rover would land safely and whether the astronauts would return to Earth unharmed. In the end, the mission was successful.

SELECTING A MATHEMATICS PROGRAM
FOR GRADES 1 AND 2

After using the *Chicago Everyday Math* program for several years, the Primary Unit team decided to look for a math curriculum that better emphasized thinking skills, was interdisciplinary, and covered fewer topics than *Chicago*. They wanted to emphasize depth over breadth. The team examined alternative programs, including *Bridges in Mathematics*, a curriculum similar to one a team member had previously used in Oregon. They compared *Bridges* with *Chicago Everyday Math, Marilyn Burns,* and *TERC.* They listed the attributes of *Bridges* and questions that needed to be answered before making a curriculum choice: How will it work in a vertically grouped class? Can we use parts if we can't finish? What can be eliminated? Can our schedule allow for the additional time required? How will we know if *Bridges* is better than *Chicago* once we use it? Can we pilot it for a year and compare outcomes?

The teachers contacted the developers of *Bridges* and asked about longitudinal research. Each team member then reviewed one of the grade-level units of study and reported back to the group. After meeting to review their findings, the team unanimously decided to purchase and pilot the *Bridges* program in all three vertically grouped classrooms.

Primary Unit teacher Janet Weinstein believed that students with significant difficulty in understanding number were not well served by any of the programs reviewed so she enrolled in Making Math Real: Multisensory Structured Methodologies for Cognitive Development in Math, a program developed and taught by David Berg, an educational therapist at Berkeley. This program involved several intensive summer courses. Janet came away convinced that using visual, auditory, and tactile methods with children who might be classified as suffering from a math disability or dyscalculia would lead to successful math achievement. She was so impressed with the results that she began using it with a few children in her classroom and eventually used it for private tutoring as she continued to study with Berg.

DESIGNING AN OUTDOOR CURRICULUM

While environmental education was a key component of the TPS program from the school's founding, it was more firmly established in the late 1980s and early 1990s through the work of Middle School teacher Chris Taranta. In 1989, in recognition of his innovative, cutting-edge work with students first at Sycamore Farm and later at Shelly Ridge, Chris received a Christa McAuliffe Fellowship, an annual award funded by Congress in memory of the science teacher who died in a tragic space shuttle accident. Chris used the award to publish a K–8 environmental science curriculum based on the work of his TPS colleagues.

To celebrate the 20th anniversary of Earth Day, Chris and his students created the "Protect Our Planet" calendar, which included illustrations and daily tips and facts to encourage preservation of the natural environment. After local publisher Running Press published and distributed the calendar nationally, our environmental education program received national and international media attention, including a feature story on *Good Morning America* and a mention on CNN International. (One of our school's founders saw the story in her hotel room while on a visit to Asia!) The calendar was also awarded the President's Environmental Youth Award. On November 14, 1990, in a ceremony at the Executive Office Building in Washington, DC, President Bush personally presented the award to Chris and one of the four students at the ceremony representing the Middle School. On January 17, 1991, Congressman William H. Gray read the following statement into the Congressional Record:

> Mr. Speaker, I want to congratulate the middle school students of the Philadelphia School in my district for winning the President's Environmental Youth Award. The school won the award for their Protect Our Planet' environmental calendar. . . . The Philadelphia School's calendar and environmental program have served as models for other schools around the nation. As we become more concerned with the fate of our Nation's natural resources, we should commend the Philadelphia School which continually seeks to invest a sense of wonder and insight about the environment in its students.

VOYAGE OF THE MIMI

In 1989, the Junior Unit faculty decided to experiment with an interdisciplinary program designed by the Bank Street College of Education.[1] With a diverse cast (including age, race, and disability status) and incorporating scientific, fictional, and computer components, the 13 episodes of *Voyage of the Mimi* featured the sea-faring adventures of Captain Granville and his crew as they studied humpback whales off the coast of Massachusetts. A highlight of the study was the Junior Unit trip to South Street Seaport in New York to visit with cast members, whom the students had followed for almost a year. (I don't recall if the students met the very young Ben Affleck, who starred in the series.) Satisfied with how each lesson related to real world applications, in 1992 the teachers used its sequel, the *Second Voyage of the Mimi*, which explored Maya civilization.

LEGO TECHNIC AND LEGO LOGO

In the 1994–95 school year, teacher Jennifer Furniss introduced Lego Technic to her co-teacher Miriam Harlan and their third graders. Jennifer had used the program previously in her classroom in England. The curriculum involved constructing a series of Lego mechanical objects that provided hands-on experience in exploring simple machines. Miriam, whose expertise was in language arts and thematic educations, was open to experimenting with this program, recognizing that the construction of the Lego objects required careful attention to detail, a skill with transfer benefit to all disciplines. The next year, as fourth graders, the students applied their knowledge of physical science to Lego Logo, a programming language that manipulated Lego constructions. A graduating eighth grader reflected on his Lego Technic experience:

> I remember Lego Technics. We would build different structures out of Legos and that would model the

1. In the early 1980s, the U.S. Department of Education put out a request for proposals for a multimedia science curriculum that would include TV, computer software, video disks, teacher guides, and other educational materials *The Voyage of the Mimi* was chosen as a recipient of the funding. The curriculum is now available online.

six simple machines-wheel and axle, gear, lever, pulley, inclined plane, and wedge. The Postage scale expressed lever. It took me a whole week to build but when I was done, I felt really proud. This past year in Middle School we studied physics, and I ran into my old friend, the lever. Now I understand lever arm and fulcrum, and physics makes sense.

FOUNDING OF THE PRESCHOOL

The opening of a preschool program for three- and four-year-olds became a reality in 2000. Its founding director was Primary Unit teacher Maureen Glaccum, who had been an early childhood educator for many years before joining the Primary Unit team. It was exciting to work alongside her as she created a brand-new program for young learners. A given for both of us was that preschool classes would be team-taught by faculty paid on the same scale at our K–8 teachers, making it possible to hire the most highly qualified early childhood educators.

Maureen designed a play-based program that supported project-based learning. For example, during the all-school theme "Benjamin Franklin," the preschoolers listened to stories about Franklin and learned about some of the Philadelphia institutions associated with him. They then transformed their classrooms into a firehouse, post office, hospital, apothecary shop, and invention workshop. Parents visited the preschool on "Ben Franklin Day," when the preschoolers, wearing three-cornered hats and bifocals, led them in candle-making and printing activities while eating scones and drinking tea. Programs such as this one connected the children with the larger school community and to the city where they lived.

Opening a new preschool was an ambitious project, and we worried that we might not achieve the enrollment numbers we sought for the first year. However, because of its outstanding faculty and program, we ended up with a long waiting list for admission. Over the next few years, we fitted out the remainder of the available space to accommodate increased enrollment.

TRUSTING TEACHERS is key to an educational program that is innovative, creative, and effective. An atmosphere of trust produces teachers who feel valued. As TPS teacher Miriam Harlan shared with me,

> I work at a school where I feel valued and valuable. I have the opportunity to create as well as implement curricula. I work with others who are similarly inclined. There are ever opportunities to learn and grow as a teacher and a human being.

CHAPTER 17

Education of Character

*The moral purpose of the school is universal and dominant
in all instruction, whatever the topic.*

John Dewey

CHARACTER DEVELOPMENT continues throughout one's lifetime, with personal, academic, and professional experiences all playing a role. Intrinsic to all learning, it is not a separate discipline to be taught in a classroom. At The Philadelphia School our educational program—in terms of philosophy, practice, and content—supported the moral development of our students.

BEING A PART OF A SCHOOL COMMUNITY

Throughout the school day the interactions between students and between students and the adults in their school community—be they faculty, administrative staff, parent volunteers, facilities personnel, or bus drivers—influence character development. As John Dewey described, in a democracy, moral education comes about in communities of individuals interacting in purposeful activities with one another.

For some students such interactions began in the early morning with Mr. Bill, our bus driver for many years. In her graduation speech, one student described how at "6:50 am, Mr. Bill's horn would tell me it was time for me to get on the bus. He would always wait patiently, sometimes even knocking on the door." Something as basic as a teacher's greeting in the schoolyard or classroom made a child feel welcome, known, and safe. Modeling such warm and caring interactions was important. Equally important was having the daily schedule on the board when students arrived in the classroom so that the children knew what to expect, giving them a sense of control and order.

Every interaction throughout the day was consequential. Teachers modeled kind, cooperative, and polite interactions between themselves as co-teachers. Their response to student work always included a comment about the content, what was appreciated and what could use more work, showing teacher interest rather than a judgmental, possibly dismissive grade. When working independently, there was a system in place by which a student could get the teacher's attention, for example, "put your name on the board and I'll get to you." Children were expected to wait their turn and not interrupt, thus learning about respecting others and about delaying gratification.

Were there disruptive students? Did children treat others unkindly? Of course. They were children. But they learned from their mistakes and from the ways they were held accountable. For example, every now and then a child just could not resist pulling the handle of a fire alarm. Charles was one such child. I asked him to come to my office afterwards and to explain what happened. Remembering that day (and never pulling the fire alarm ever again), Charles later wrote, "Sandy taught me not to draw conclusions or to make judgements before you know the whole story and all of the facts. She also showed me the value of listening."

Whenever a student was sent to my office for misbehavior in class, such as disruption of a lesson, I had them write a note about the incident for their parent to sign and return. A typical response from a first grader, in invented spelling, went like this:

I'm sorry if you haven't herd the best from me but that's going to change. Ther's going to be know more clown-

ing! Your not going to hear bad things from me AGAIN!!
I'm going to be a whole new Diego. Love Diego

From time to time, there was a need to have regularly scheduled meetings with a particular group of children—perhaps a
whole grade or a group of boys or girls. Issues of inclusion and
exclusion, fairness, handling conflict, and tolerance of individual
differences were predictable among preadolescent girls. Regular
meetings gave the girls the opportunity to develop strategies for
conflict resolution other than the habit of silencing oneself or
turning away from conflict altogether.

The fifth-grade girls, each year, it seemed, often had disagreements arising from a "best friend" telling another girl in the
group a secret or from a child struggling to be part of a group.
I facilitated regular meetings with them (sometimes with our
school psychologist), during which each one was able to express
their point of view without interruption, and then we attempted
to find solutions. In one especially contentious year, the girls
decided to write a play about their difficulties. Interestingly, in
their script the children expressed their belief that the more parents became involved in trying to solve their disputes, the worse
the outcome. They understood that there was benefit in finding
solutions themselves as a group.

From many of these conversations, though, it was evident
that many preadolescents simply could not put themselves in
each other's shoes. Empathy was not yet reliably present in
their social-emotional toolbox. I remember clearly when two
third-grade girls, one in tears, were sent to my office. The sob-
bing child told me that the other child, her best friend, had told
her that her sweater was ugly. I asked the "perpetrator" how she
would feel if I told her that her sweater was ugly. She replied that
she was fine with that because she knew her sweater was not ugly
and maintained that her friend shouldn't be upset because it was
the truth—her sweater was ugly.

It takes time and patience for children to develop the sensitiv-
ity to know when it is best to not say anything rather than utter a

perceived truth that may be hurtful. We knew that it was important to take time to deal with these everyday squabbles. It was all
part of learning to live with each other. Direct response to these
situations when they arose was certainly necessary, but it was
equally important that such values as kindness, empathy, and
fairness were supported by a curriculum that did not shy away
from exploring them through history, literature, and the arts.

CHARACTER EDUCATION THROUGH CONTENT

Empathy, coupled with critical thinking, is fundamental to
understanding and undoing social injustice and inequity. Classrooms must be settings for examining America's unvarnished
history, for discussing the ongoing fight for civil and human
rights, and for taking action to create a more perfect nation. This
stance sadly is in direct opposition to the message being legis-
lated in many states today: that our children must be protected
from the study of history and literature related to Indigenous
and Black history, social injustice, racism, and LGBTQ+ rights.

In a recent interview, a teacher in Utah told me that whenever
he was creating material for student use, the computer would
flag a "sensitive" topic and alert the administration. Teachers
were told to avoid controversial or political topics. For example, the words "equity" and "consent" would be flagged, and the
teacher warned. All books need to be approved by a school committee, which included parents. Parents had always had the right
to exempt their own child from reading a book that they felt
was inappropriate, but now books are banned for all children.
On a somewhat more hopeful note, a public school teacher in
Portland, Oregon, having read about the teacher's experience in
Utah, wrote me the following:

> It absolutely breaks my heart to hear about the teacher
> in Utah. It is night and day from here. My school is very
> inclusive of all student identities—there are visual and
> verbal messages of inclusion around race, religion, sexual
> orientation, etc. everywhere. I fear that we're becoming a

country where the only freedom in some states pertains to buying guns.

School boards have been increasingly influenced by intolerant extremists. Moms for Liberty, an organization founded in January 2021, accuses teachers of using books to indoctrinate kids about critical race theory and gender fluidity. With more than 240 chapters in 42 states and more than 100,000 members, Moms for Liberty members attend board meetings to challenge curriculum. In Williamson County, Tennessee, in 2021, Moms for Liberty challenged a carefully selected K–8 interdisciplinary language arts curriculum, *Wit and Wisdom*. They urged the board to eliminate more than 30 books, including *Martin Luther King, Jr. and the March on Washington* (Penguin Young Readers, Level 3) because, among other reasons, it contained photographs of firefighters hosing Black Americans. These vocal women did not even have children in the school district.[1]

Harvard Professor Emeritus Robert Coles believes that the most powerful way we learn morals is through stories—through literature and history.[2] The humanities intrinsically are a pathway toward learning about the human condition. Still relevant today, Coles argued the following in a lecture at Harvard many years ago:

> You need an education that in some way will help you to walk in the shoes of others and not only try to pull other

---

1. In the November 2022 mid-term elections, Moms for Liberty endorsed and actively supported like-minded candidates running for school boards across the country, but fortunately the nonpartisan election site Ballotpedia's analysis of 361 school board elections saw a rejection of these candidates. Ballotpedia found that only about 36% of candidates who opposed diversity initiatives or the use of gender-neutral learning materials won their elections.

2. Robert Coles, *The Call of Stories: Teaching and the Moral Imagination* (Boston: Houghton Mifflin, 1989). Robert Coles is the author of numerous books, including his series *Children of Crisis*, for which he won a Pulitzer Prize. He has also won a MacArthur Award, a Presidential Medal of Freedom, and a National Humanities Medal.

people into your shoes. . . . let us make common cause around some knowledge of what it is that both unites us and separates us. How do we try to reach out to others, link arms with them, work with them, without the singular risks of condescension, of blindness, where we fail not only to see what is happening to ourselves, but also to others? Education is being shaken up, derailed, from those tracks we get onto, with all the certainties, sometimes the false certainties, they offer us—the stages, phases, categories, definition, mandates, rules—marching us through anything so that we tame uncertainty, ambiguity, and contradiction—the very stuff of life.[3]

Through our thematic curriculum—with literature and history at its core—students delved into a wide range of social and moral situations. With their teachers, they explored topics in depth, gaining insight into issues confronting their world. One parent perfectly summed up where a theme could lead:

To me [the theme] Coal Mining was the quintessential example about how whenever you study a subject in depth you find it is hooked up to everything else in the universe. Through coal mining, Mary Beth gained empathy for the lives of coal miners and their children. She learned about immigration and why people leave one place for another and what sort of problems they run into. She learned about geology and how the earth's layers are formed. She learned about energy sources and why they are important. She learned wonderful songs about coal miners and built her own beautiful coal mine, peat bog, and coal museum. Finally, she got to ride down into the earth and experience the world underground. The whole unit gave her so many new insights.

3. I saved this quote for many years because it is so compelling. Unfortunately, I no longer have a citation for it, although I believe it is from a lecture for Harvard's Gen Ed 105 class in the 1970s.

Another example was the Junior Unit's study of the Civil Rights Movement of the 1950s and 1960s, a time in our nation's history that touches an emotional chord. Students explored how social change came about from court cases, boycotts, sit-ins, and marches. They looked for examples of the indignities and violence that often were the response to the movement's nonviolent approach. Specifically, students examined the 13th, 14th, and 15th amendments; *Plessy v Ferguson* and *Brown v Board of Education*; the desegregation of Central High School in Little Rock, the Montgomery bus boycott, and lunch counter sit-ins in Nashville. They watched and discussed the award-winning documentary series *Eyes on the Prize*, which traces the history of the civil rights movement. Students read Christopher Paul Curtis's novel *The Watsons Go to Birmingham—1963*, which tells the story of a Black family's road trip from their home in Michigan to Alabama, where they witness a tragic event in American history. The Junior Unit traveled to Washington, DC, to see exhibits at the Smithsonian Museum of American Art on the Great Migration of African Americans from the south to the north and on the 50th anniversary of *Brown v Board of Education*. Their study of the Civil Rights Movement culminated with the student-written, multi-media production "Shards of Glass," which represented Black struggles following the Civil War and the fight for civil rights. After the performance, one of our parents, a Black professor, sent us this note:

> Thank you for showing your courage, heart, and dedication toward the Civil War Period in America. . . . I appreciate your heart, confidence, and guts for presenting this information to the public. These kids presented an important facet of the life that most African Americans have never witnessed in the U.S. Perhaps, many non-blacks have never seen a production of this nature either. Congratulations to you for accepting the challenge!

Exposure to compelling content—asking and trying to answer complicated questions orally and in writing—is critical for moral development. Our students were encouraged to stand in the shoes of people they never met, often ordinary people struggling to make this a better world. But, of course, despite this emphasis, there was an occasional disconnect between a student's intellectual response to this material and their behavior. I recall an incident when a student in the Junior Unit was subjected to teasing by first a few and then increasing numbers of classmates; eventually virtually every classmate participated in the harassment, which ultimately became physical. One student stepped up and "blew the whistle." Teachers immediately put a stop to the behavior, facilitated self-examination by the students, and implemented sanctions.

Thus, despite being a school viewed by its community as a place where the "kids are not mean," harassment occurred, and this incident taught us that constant vigilance and attention to our community was necessary to maintain a kind and caring environment. I often asked the following question to students experiencing conflict: "If we can't find a way to get along and to care for each other in this nurturing environment, how can we expect governments or countries to find common ground?"

A MORAL COMPASS

Children as young as preschoolers were encouraged to consider making choices guided by a moral compass. They were encouraged to resolve conflicts over a toy by taking turns. To accelerate their advance from parallel play to playing together, preschoolers were encouraged to work together, for example, to build a structure and to listen to one another. Preschool teacher Maureen Glaccum read the fairy tale *Rumpelstiltskin* to the children and asked them whether it was okay for the miller's daughter to break her promise to give Rumpelstiltskin her first child. This discussion was a prelude to the discussions they had in Junior Unit and Middle School about civil disobedience as practiced by Mohandas Gandhi and Martin Luther King. Students were asked to consider if it was justified to break the law when India broke with Great Britain and, if so, why. Today we might ask students to compare the January 6, 2021, insurrection with the sit-ins and boycotts in the South during the 1960s.

INTERDEPENDENCE

Children learn social responsibility when they are given opportunities for engagement with their school community, their city, and the world. At a small school like TPS, team sports played a large role in fostering a sense of interdependence; everyone on the team was needed and there could be little dependence on star players. Children needed to become aware of and respect each other's strengths and weaknesses. Throughout the course of their time at TPS, all students took part in several theme-related plays and musicals, ranging from *Really Rosie* to *Romeo and Juliet*, and depended on each other to learn lines, build the set, make props, and provide musical accompaniment. By working together on science projects, theme projects, gardening, fort-building, and other collaborative activities, children regularly made decisions that required compromise, turn taking, and conflict resolution.

HELPING THE SCHOOL COMMUNITY

Caring is a key ingredient of civic engagement. Children need opportunities to help others—and to experience the rewards of helping others. Each student at The Philadelphia School was responsible for an age-appropriate classroom or school community job. Our youngest children rotated classrooms jobs, such as being line leader, delivering the milk cartons at lunchtime, and wiping down tables after lunch. To make sure everyone was included, they walked to recess in the park with an assigned partner and rotated their seating at lunchtime. Junior Unit and Middle School students provided school-wide assistance, for example, washing paintbrushes in the art room, recycling, and helping in the preschool during lunchtime.

HELPING BEYOND TPS

Service initiatives were often inspired by societal problems of which students became aware as part of their studies. Most social service agencies and other nonprofits in the Philadelphia area offered on-site community service opportunities to children only high-school age and older. Because of this, most service activities took place at the school. For example, when the third grade explored the idea of how one person can make a difference, the children took part in the fund-raising Read to Feed read-athon for the nonprofit Heifer International, which provides livestock and training to subsistence farmers in Asia and Africa. The children had the opportunity to choose which animals to purchase with the funds they raised. Here are some their reflections on the power of taking action:

> "We can make people's lives a lot better, so they don't suffer."
> "We are helping children in need."
> "I learned you can help people get animals by reading and animals help people."
> "I learned there are a lot more poor kids than I thought."
> "We can change the world for them."

Service opportunities included preparing Monday supper each week for residents of a nearby shelter for men experiencing homelessness; surveying neighborhood street trees for the Center City Greening Project; conserving new plant growth and removing exotic plants in sensitive areas of Fairmount Park; and distributing window-box plants grown by inmates at Graterford Prison.[4]

4. The children wrote thank you cards to the men participating in the greenhouse program. The following response was sent to the students by the prisoners' counselor: "The men participating in the Graterford greenhouse program were touched by the effort, sentiments, and energetic artwork. Each card was passed around the table and each was like a light of hope from and connection to the normal world outside of the bleak prison environment."

Each year the Student Council spearheaded several fund raisers (often in the form of ever-popular bake sales) for local, national, and international causes. They also organized book and food drives. Their annual run-, walk-, bike-athon raised financial aid funds for children attending TPS. Shortly before I left TPS, the parents association organized "First Week" drives to help meet the needs of a variety of local nonprofits; the idea was to sponsor monthly service initiatives that were visible to the children on a regular basis in the front hallway of the school.

LEARNING TO SELF-ADVOCATE AND ADVOCATE FOR OTHERS

Self-advocacy is the ability to communicate your needs. Individuals who know how to advocate for themselves and others are empowered to find solutions to personal and societal problems. No child is too young to have opportunities to advocate for themselves and others, and classrooms should nurture the development of student advocacy.

Students often presented petitions to me with specific requests regarding a variety of issues. While I did not always agree with their requests, I did take them seriously. One of the easier ones to respond to was a request for a "snowball license." Our children loved to play in the snow at recess time in the nearby playground. They were only allowed to throw snowballs if they were issued a license to do so. Hence the following request:

Dear Sandy Dean,

On the behalf of JU-A [4th and 5th grades] I would like to ask that the JU-A students be allowed to throw snowballs during the winter of 2004–05. We would only hit each other from our shoulders down. We would be as responsible as we could be and still have fun. Remember last year? We received a license but it never snowed hard enough to make snowballs.

License was granted.

One year I received the following petition signed by 24 eighth graders.

Dear Sandy:

As you may know, during Mini-Courses this year, the eighth graders will be preparing *The Play Called Noah's Flood* in drama class to be performed in March. Though we are very excited about the upcoming play, we have been informed that we will be required to attend eleven drama classes per week during mini-courses, two each day and three on Friday.

As eighth graders, we are very concerned about this scheduling. From our understanding, the purpose of mini-courses is to give us a chance to explore areas of our culture that we would not be able to do otherwise. In fact, this year, our last year of mini-course, we will not get a chance to participate in mini-courses that we did not get to participate in the previous years. After adding up the eleven periods of drama, drug education, SSR periods, Latin, book groups, chorus, and check-out, we may only have the chance to take only three elective mini-courses, or less.

Many of us have relatively small parts in the play, and, while we are not dissatisfied with our roles, many of us will be spending much of the twenty-two hours of drama during mini-courses with not much to do.

We are well aware that there has been a problem with the efficiency of our work, and we will do our best to try to deal with our talking, while keeping our enthusiasm high without getting out of hand. We also understand that a large amount of time and planning went into the scheduling of drama periods, and that a lot of mini-courses were scheduled around drama. However, we would be very grateful if you would consider minimizing the amount of drama classes during mini-courses, perhaps to six per week instead of eleven. Thank you for your time and consideration.

I am happy to report that the students did achieve a scheduling compromise between the drama teacher and their classroom teachers, and *The Play Called Noah's Flood* was a success. The students' self-advocacy not only helped solve a problem but also reminded me how much they valued mini-courses.[5]

Petitions did not always result in a change, but the students were always heard. Every now and then I received student requests for a school dance. Here is a note I received from a sixth grader:

> Dear Sandy,
>
> May I ask you a question? Why don't we have a Valentine's Day dance, or a dance for any other occasion? Students can work together by planning the music, decorations, food, etc. I hope you will think about this and maybe bring it up in a student council meeting.
>
> Thank you for listening.
>
> Rebecca
> 6th grade student

I turned down this request, explaining that I believed that school dances for middle schoolers were not developmentally appropriate for all children.[6]

---

5. In late February or early March, the Middle School teachers, including specialists, set aside their usual curriculum to offer three weeks of mini-courses, elective courses that in 2003–04 included Badminton, Bridge, Cooking for a Local Shelter, Dissection, French, Hip Hop and Jazz Dance, Jewelry-making, Mideastern Current Events, Origami, Protest Music, Science Teaching, and Solar Cars. Middle schoolers taught some of the mini-courses themselves. Required mini-courses included Book Group, Prep for Theme Plays, and Decisions (topics, in alternating years, related to sexual health and substance abuse).

6. School dances for many middle schoolers are painful experiences, especially for some of the boys, who often dealt with their anxiety by unruly behavior. I had attended enough bar and bat mitzvahs of TPS seventh graders to know what often occurred. There was no reason for our school to rush children into social situations before they were ready.

Learning to speak up for oneself is a first step toward advocating for concerns that go beyond one's own interests. Students benefit immeasurably from a school setting in which teachers celebrate student voices and listen and respond to student opinions and concerns. They learn what it means to be a citizen of a community through active, meaningful daily interactions, compelling academic content, and opportunities for self-expression. In this way, students develop a sense of how individuals ought to treat one another with kindness, empathy, humility, and compassion.

CHAPTER 18

Democracy Is Central

Part of what we have to do a better job of, if our democracy is to function in a complicated diverse society like this, is to teach our kids enough critical thinking to be able to sort out what is true and what is false, what is contestable and what is incontestable.

President Barack Obama

IN 1888, JOHN DEWEY described democracy as a "form of government only because it is a form of moral and spiritual association."[1] More than 100 years later, in a New York *Times* opinion essay published, upon his request, shortly after his death, Congressman John Lewis wrote, "Democracy is not a state. It is an act, and each generation must do its part to help build what we called the Beloved Community, a nation and world society at peace with itself.[2]

Throughout each chapter of this book, I have tried to weave, explicitly or implicitly, Dewey's view of democracy as civic-minded participation by individuals who, understanding the wants and needs of others, are able to cooperate, collaborate,

---

1. *The Ethics of Democracy*, in the *Collected Works of John Dewey* (Early Works, vol. 1, p. 240), Southern Illinois University Press, 2008.

2. https://www.nytimes.com/2020/07/30/opinion/john-lewis-civil-rights-america.html

and compromise to meet the challenges of an ever-changing world. I want to go a little deeper here to describe how we educated children for democratic participation by creating conditions that enabled them to make meaning over time out of real experiences.

There is a lot of talk these days of the need for teaching civics in American schools, but learning about the three branches of government or how a bill is passed in Congress, for example, is insufficient for understanding what it means to live in a democratic society. Students need to understand what a democracy requires of its citizens. They need opportunities to explore all the various ways of interacting—listening carefully to other points of view, realizing when they are hurting the feelings of others or feeling hurt themselves and appreciating the consequences of each, working through inevitable conflicts that occur among members of a group, recognizing and respecting people's differences (ethnicity, religion, gender, sexual preference, class, culture), and understanding universal commonalities (need for love, inclusion, security, justice, recognition, success).

At The Philadelphia School we considered democracy as an ethical concept. Our classrooms were settings for modeling respectful speaking and listening, and participatory roles for students were built into school life, community service, and social advocacy projects. These real-life situations required students to work cooperatively and to reflect on the need for compromise. As students moved through the grades, they often worked in pairs or small groups to complete a task or solve a problem, with the tasks getting more complex as the children grew older. Students listened to and adopted each other's ideas. They learned to recognize each other's strengths and weaknesses and took increasing responsibility for their own learning and for helping with others' learning. Teachers created opportunities for students to reflect on and to discuss ideas and issues. Our practices of displaying all students' work and having students share their writings with their classmates were intentional, organized ways of "hearing" everybody's ideas. The disconnect between exploring the concept of empathy and behaving in ways that are decidedly unempathetic, as exemplified in the Junior Unit incident described in the previous chapter, was in and of itself a learning opportunity for children.

The goal of educating for life in a democratic society shaped our practice of creating conditions where students made meaning of historical, literary, and other sources to understand from multiple perspectives the broad and vital themes of human history, social systems, and multiple cultures. Such themes include people's capacity for altruism or selfishness, construction or destruction, justice or injustice, inclusion or bigotry, and change and continuity. Our thematic approach combined the social sciences with the humanities, providing the knowledge and opportunities to explore these dichotomies.

Perhaps it is apt that the quote "Tradition is not the worship of the ashes but the passing on of the fire" is attributed variously to three consequential figures—Thomas More, Benjamin Franklin, and Gustav Mahler. History consists of a tension between continuity and change. Educating for democracy requires that its virtues not be taken for granted and its fragility be recognized. Focusing history and social studies on broad themes and questions, approached from multiple perspectives, provides opportunities for children to internalize the habits of open-minded and critical judgment based on evidence. Whenever possible, teachers at The Philadelphia School used original sources, rather than relying on a textbook version of "fact" without context. This approach required that teachers develop curricula that went beyond providing dates and facts for students to memorize; this took time, research, energy, and creativity—as well as a heavy-duty copying machine for teacher use.

Guiding participatory classroom activities that explore in depth themes and issues of historical and social experience consumed time and energy that might have otherwise been devoted to covering more subject matter. Affective and critical thinking over a limited range of topics, facts, and ideas, however, can advance the development of optimistic citizens who recognize the inequities and imperfections of our world and are prepared to engage in social action as adults to improve matters. That is an effort worth doing.

In their mid-year and end-of-year curriculum summaries, teachers captured the essence of our progressive practice as described above. The following excerpt from a curriculum summary for the Middle School thematic study "Uruk to Athens: Learning from Ancient Civilizations," demonstrates what "lesson planning" looked like at The Philadelphia School. I chose this particular unit of study because it directly relates to democratic values—and threats to these values in the past and present.

> *Unit Study:* Uruk to Athens: Learning from Ancient
>   Civilizations
> *Concepts:* culture, cultural change, customs, democracy
> *Main ideas:* A culture may be defined by the behaviors,
>   beliefs, customs, and attitudes of a group of people. A cul-
>   ture's values are reflected in the artwork, the literature,
>   the language, the inventions, and traditions of the people.
>   We have benefited from the accomplishments of human
>   beings reaching back thousands of years. The forces that
>   cause cultures to flourish, to change, or to vanish are the
>   concerns of this study. Today we live in a world of many
>   cultures—a multicultural world. We have learned from
>   civilizations in all parts of the world, and we continue to
>   interact with other cultural groups. We are linked to the
>   cultures of the past, just as cultures of the future will be
>   linked to us. All people, past and present, have shaped
>   their beliefs and behavior in the face of universal human
>   needs and problems. The various elements of any culture
>   are interrelated and cannot be understood without exam-
>   ining the entirety of the culture. The culture of any society
>   is constantly being altered, and a change in one element
>   will affect changes in other elements.
> *Specific knowledge:* Students identified the factors and events
>   that allowed Athens to transition into a partial democracy

in the 6th century BCE and how that form of government relates to democracy in the United States today, with special attention paid to the presidential election.

Application of knowledge: During their study of democracy, students participated in a simulated Athenian Ekklesia (Assembly); they created a Greek persona, wrote a persuasive speech championing a political or social issue, and debated on behalf of their position.

Activities: While comparing Athenian and American democracy, students examined the electoral votes controlled by each state and made predictions about the 2004 election.

If we truly want an educated population capable of functioning as competent citizens in our democracy, we must give students the skills and the opportunity to wrestle with complicated and controversial issues.

CHAPTER 19

Multiculturalism and Addressing Racism

In the end, there is only one race: the human race.
Josephine Baker

JOSEPHINE BAKER'S WORDS aptly describe our school's approach in the late 1980s and 1990s to addressing racism. As a small school with a low student-to-teacher ratio, a strong advisory system, and a focus on the whole child, we believed that we knew all our children well and were meeting their individual needs. Philosophically we maintained that nurturing the development of critical thinking skills and empathy would cultivate students who championed anti-racism. In a June 2022 *Washington Post* interview, scholar and author Ibram X. Kendi affirmed this stance, saying, "to be racist is to be a believer, and to be anti-racist is to be a thinker." He added, "I think it is incredibly important to ask questions of our children, not just to model critical thinking but also to raise empathy, to encourage a child to be empathetic."[1]

As mentioned earlier, we believed that the practice of using primary sources to focus on broad themes and questions, from

1. https://www.washingtonpost.com/lifestyle/2022/06/14/ibram-x-kendi-how-to-raise-an-antiracist/

a multicultural lens of multiple perspectives, was more effective than relying on short-lived memorization of a textbook's version of "facts" without context. This approach provided an opportunity for children to internalize the habits of open-minded and critical judgment based on evidence—habits vital for lives of personal integrity as citizens of a democratic society.

MULTICULTURALISM

Our curriculum explored multiple perspectives, took a critical look at our nation's history, and included the experiences of people of color. We pursued what we called a "multicultural curriculum," approaching all areas of study in a manner so as to understand the diverse strands that for so long have made up our nation's communities, culture, traditions, values, and achievements. The history of Blacks in the United States was threaded throughout the curriculum, and immigration featured prominently in our curricula.

No school can pursue an in-depth study of each and every ethnic group in our nation, much less the world. Schools can, however, explore overarching, universal conceptual issues, such as conflict and resolution, regardless of the topic of study. This conceptual structure also fostered an approach that took into consideration multiple perspectives. As mentioned in an earlier chapter, no study of 1492 is complete without an awareness of the points of view of the Native Americans, the European explorers, the Spanish crown, and the Catholic Church. A study of the American Constitution is incomplete without discussing the 3/5 compromise and why it came about. Recognizing the reasons behind immigration to the United States—reasons shared by immigrants from our nation's earliest days up to today—prepares students to understand and empathize with the experiences of displaced peoples across the globe. Equally important was learning about the Great Migration, the movement of Black Americans from farms in the South to cities in the North; a compelling resource was the book *The Great Migration*, based on a series of paintings by Jacob Lawrence.

Our commitment to Spanish language study, from preschool through eighth grade, was grounded in the belief that by studying a second language at an early age, children develop an awareness and openness to other cultures. They learn about the people and countries where the language is spoken—including the history, traditions, customs, and geography of those countries. Students acquire a more global perspective and develop an early understanding of the relationship between cultures and languages. In the spring of their eighth-grade year, students traveled outside the continental United States to a Spanish-speaking region of the world. One alumnus, who now practices international law in D.C., credited his TPS trip to Cuba in 2003 as the catalyst for his love of travel and his acquisition of several languages. In a 2009–10 survey of TPS alumni, more than 60 percent reported that they used Spanish regularly in their academic and professional lives.

Our interdisciplinary thematic curriculum was multicultural in nature. Our youngest children studied other countries and cultures with the goal of helping them understand, by comparison, their own culture and world. The children discovered they belong to many groups: religious, cultural, geographic, gender-based, racial, and economic. Topics of study, which varied from year to year, focused on India, China, Italy, Africa, and pre-colonial North America. When the topic was not directly related to other cultures, we included the contributions and experiences of women and people of color. For example, a study of the history of flight would not be complete without acknowledging the contributions of Beryl Markham and Amelia Earhart; nor would a study of American inventors, without mention of Elijah ("the real") McCoy and Charles Drew.

The thematic American history curriculum for grades 3 to 5 included many of the topics currently being banned by local school boards across the country, for example, the deleterious impact of European colonization on Native American tribes, the treatment of Chinese workers on the Transcontinental Railroad, Jim Crow; and the Civil Rights movement of the 1950s and

1960s. Students considered the Declaration of Independence's proclamation that "all men are created equal" within the context of Black enslavement. They learned that the phrase has over time slowly become more inclusive, but that there remains a difference between the ideal and reality. Students focused on what produces conflict, the methods used to resolve conflict, and how different groups developed different approaches to common concerns. The curriculum explored the stories and experiences of marginalized and oppressed groups through literature, art, and music.

The Middle School's three-year theme rotation was essentially Eurocentric, but its foundation was conceptual, with students considering issues of power, oppression, liberty, and justice. The curriculum focused on Western ideas and experiences because of their influence on the development of the cultural, economic, and governmental structure of the United States. Students in grades 6 to 8 looked at the impact of European colonizers throughout history, with an introduction to concurrent civilizations of Asia and Africa. Independent research projects gave middle schoolers the opportunity to pursue topics of individual interest, many of which focused on non-Western subjects or ethnic oppression, such as 15th-century tribal life in Kenya, chivalry and bushido, the Ming Dynasty, gold and slave trade routes, Mansa Musa, and the Spanish Inquisition.

The three-week mini-course session for middle schoolers included courses designed to examine issues of ethnicity, prejudice, discrimination, liberation, empowerment, and advancement in modern society. Each student was a member of a book group and could choose from such titles as *The Diary of Anne Frank*, *The Autobiography of Malcom X*, Harper Lee's *To Kill a Mockingbird*, Bette Greene's *The Summer of My German Soldier*, William Heath's *The Children Bob Moses Led*, and Camille Yarbrough's *Shimmershine Queens*. One year, I led a group reading Lois Lowry's *The Giver*, which is about a dystopia where citizens were not given freedom or choice, including occupation and level of education, with the goal of eliminating poverty and war. My students happened to be from diverse socio-economic backgrounds, and there was a fascinating exchange of ideas among them. The more privileged students rejected the society, which they viewed as dystopian. The more economically disadvantaged students thought the society was utopian because it worked better for most people, and, thus, they were willing to relinquish freedom of choice. The children openly discussed their biases.

ADDRESSING SYSTEMIC RACISM

Even though our multicultural curriculum was, I believe, well in advance of the programs at many other schools, by the early 2000s in was clear that our efforts were not enough in addressing systemic racism. As enrollment of students of color increased, many of their parents began to voice concern that we were not providing the support needed for their children to thrive. Our faculty began to gradually diversify, with new, young teachers whose lived experiences and recent undergraduate and graduate work brought new perspectives to our community. They challenged our assumptions and practices. And, to be honest, it was a shock to our system.

We became increasingly aware of blind spots regarding racism in our educational program, specifically our own inability to put ourselves in the shoes of children of color (and their families) as they experienced school life in a majority white school located in a majority white neighborhood. We paid insufficient attention to the daily societal offenses experienced by people of color, and we were not cognizant of our own biases and unintentional microaggressions. We had good intentions, but good intentions were not enough.

I had believed that our multicultural curriculum, our small school size, and our progressive practice would allow us—faculty and students alike—to openly wrestle with and discuss any issues that confronted our community. We had prided ourself on viewing every student as an individual, not as one of a group. It was not that we were colorblind but rather believed strongly that what we had in common was more important than our differences. Terms such as "white privilege," "structural racism," and "microaggression" were not yet part of the general lexicon in educational circles—or even in diversity work. Psychologist Peggy McIntosh had introduced the term "white privilege" in 1989, but the concept didn't take hold in academia until nearly a dozen years later. NAIS's People of Color Conference, today a vital support system for teachers of color, was not founded until the early 1990s. Despite Kendi's affirming words about the importance of critical thinking and empathy in raising and educating anti-racists, the furtherance and implementation of diversity, equity, and inclusion work are essential.

Growing attention in the academic and public arenas to the daily and lifelong experiences of racism and discrimination shone a light on the long-standing omission of the histories, contributions, and concerns of marginalized communities (Native American, Black, Latino, Asian, LGBTQ+) not only in curricula but also in popular culture, public policy, and politics. Increased attention was being paid to the persistent ills of racism, homophobia, and misogyny. Addressing issues of social injustice and inequity has come to the fore in progressive education, and rightly so. This important work, as with any element of a curriculum, needs a solid, conceptional foundation based on intellectual, social-emotional considerations. Schools must look inward and unpack and unlearn paradigms rooted in the past.

In service of that work, I want to describe a few of the diversity efforts and challenges that characterized our school in the 1990s up until my departure after the 2005–2006 academic year.

In 1994, the school established its first Parent Diversity Committee. Its monthly meetings were attended by me, the director of admissions, and the director of development. The initial focus was increasing diversity among both faculty and students. At that time, 17% of our faculty and staff were people of color; the percentage for students was 24% (biracial, Asian-American, Black, and Latino).

Hiring teachers of color, particularly those with training or experience in progressive pedagogy, was a challenge. A strategy I employed was asking that teacher-training programs place student teachers of color at TPS. I subsequently hired some students who had been placed with us by Penn's Graduate School of Education. Unfortunately, Temple University's more diverse teacher-training program would not place their students with us because many of our teachers were not state certified (many had been but let their certification lapse). In 1997 the Klingenstein Center and the National Association of Independent Schools surveyed 500 teachers of color at independent schools to study the factors impacting recruitment and retention. The most frequent responses to the question "What makes a school attractive to teachers of color?" were the following: diversity of faculty, diversity of students, school atmosphere, school's commitment to diversity, faculty autonomy and voice, and compensation.[2]

An understandable challenge in hiring and retaining teachers of color was expressed in a heartbreaking yet inspiring letter I received from a gifted Black teacher, a woman whom I adored and respected. After teaching at TPS for a short time, she informed me of her decision to leave us at the end of the school year.

> I need to go to bed at night and know that I've done something of value that day. That's why I went into teaching. What's more important than the future of our children. . . . Maybe I will come back to TPS one day but for now I want to work with poor black children, children who have been neglected, abused, unloved and who are taught by example that hitting, fighting, and violence can make it right again.

I mourned the loss of this teacher but understood and supported her decision.

Increasing the number of students of color, particularly Black and Latino children, was a priority for the Parent Diversity Com-

2. https://www.nais.org/magazine/independent-school/fall-1999/attracting-and-retaining-teachers-of-color/

mittee. In hindsight, I realize that it was not easy for the committee's parents of color to share their children's experience with us, white administrators. After a meeting at which one parent advocated for increased Black enrollment because her child told her she wished she were white and had straight hair, the parent felt that her feelings had not been validated or accepted. Despite her continued participation in the committee's work, in the end she wrote me, "I no longer feel comfortable with sharing my daughter's experiences and will attempt to minimize them as much as possible."

In the final years of my time at TPS, the Parent Diversity Committee adopted a reading group format to discuss racism; we read Nell Painter's *Sojourner Truth: A Life, A Symbol*, James McBride's *The Color of Water*, and Julia Alvarez's *How Puerto Rican Girls Lost Their Accents*. The committee hoped that through shared reading we would create an atmosphere where all participants could speak more freely and feel heard.

Attempts to address issues of racism among the faculty and staff were often clumsy. We brought in diversity consultants to lead workshops, but—perhaps because the field was relatively new—they were not as effective as I would have liked. The workshops felt "packaged," not tailored to our teaching community. There was a lot of tiptoeing around conversations related to race. White teachers were afraid to appear to be racists and were hesitant to reflect on some of their own practices, and our few teachers of color were understandably reluctant to speak up as "representatives of their race" in large- and small-group mixed-race settings.

In 2004, I suggested at a faculty meeting that we disaggregate our standardized and classroom test data by race to look for patterns and to see who fell in the lowest quartile. A sudden hush descended on what was usually a meeting awash in diverse opinions. Everyone seemed to be afraid to speak. After some prodding on my part, the teachers shared that they assumed that the Black and Latino students would be in the lowest quartile. But this was not the case; in fact, there was greater disparity within groups than between groups. My intent was to make sure that our students receiving financial aid—most of whom were white—were succeeding. These children did not have the cultural capital that many full-paying students arrived with; if the data showed they were not doing as well as their well-resourced classmates, we were planning to address the situation. It took several meetings before we could openly and honestly look at the facts. The test data were not the only revelations at this staff meeting; it was clear that white teachers were afraid to appear racist, our few teachers of color were uncomfortable speaking up about race among their white colleagues, and almost everyone assumed that disaggregating test scores would place children of color in the lowest quartile.

In 2005 an incident in the public playground that our children used daily for recess sparked another racial controversy. A few of our younger students told their parents that Black children not from our school, perhaps truant middle schoolers, were teasing and harassing them at the playground. After looking into the situation—talking to the students and to the teachers who were on recess duty that day—we determined that nothing serious had taken place. I communicated this to the families in writing, adding that perhaps we should have more concern over the fact that the truant children were missing school. On a subsequent day, the same Black children were again in the playground. White teachers on recess duty called 911 to report the truancy. The police arrived, grabbed the boys, handcuffed them, and took them away in the back of a police car. This behavior by the police shocked everybody except our Black teachers, Black parents, and Black middle schoolers. The white teachers who had reported the truancy had thought they were doing the right thing, and they had no idea that the police would arrest the children. Many of our teachers of color viewed the teachers' call to the police as overtly racist. What was clear to me and other white teachers and staff was that we were oblivious to the reality of that level of racial injustice in the lives of our own Black students. Despite many conversations about this incident—among the faculty and with the children who witnessed the arrests—we never came to a full reconciliation during my remaining time as head of school.

This divisiveness, of course, impacted students as well. As mentioned earlier, the three-year teacher-student advisory relationship was a hallmark of the Middle School program. After the "park incident" (as it became known), students of color whose advisors were white gravitated to teachers of color who were not their advisors. Their relationship with their advisors was diminished, and this weakened the advisory system and saddened the teachers affected. One long-time white teacher, herself the parent of three adopted children of color as well as a veteran of the Civil Rights Movement in the 1960s, wrote to me about the difficult year she had just experienced. Here is an excerpt from her letter.

> Today in study hall I overheard this conversation—student one said to student two (both Black)—"I used to think that I could talk to any teacher about anything, but this year I discovered that I could only talk to [the middle school teachers of color]." That, in a nutshell, explains why this has been one of the most awful teaching years that I can remember.

The two teachers of color organized a group for Middle School students of color. This created hard feelings among white students who felt left out and wanted to be close to teachers who, in their esteem, were "cool and hip." (The two teachers were a few decades younger than their teaching teammates.) Affinity groups by race for middle school students make me uncomfortable; I question whether participating in an affinity group at this age is always developmentally appropriate. Adolescents have many grievances, and I worry that some may be framed as racial discrimination when in fact it is the universal issue of adolescents finding and developing an identity. Race is certainly a major factor but only one aspect of a child's identity. Yet I recognize that we all benefit from interactions with people who share common identities or experiences. When you are in the numerical minority of a larger community, these types of bonding inter-actions might be possible only within an affinity group. There is ongoing research about affinity groups for students of color, and I look forward to reading the findings.

I believe that affinity groups organized by interests, rather than by ethnic or racial identity, can be an effective method of exposing differing attitudes and opinions, thereby enhancing understanding of differences. Students discussing novels together, learning dances and music of various communities, working on academic projects together, joining a chorus or music ensemble, and playing sports foster community, interdependence, and trust.

A Philadelphia-area educator, Bartley Jeannoute, recently expressed it this way to me: There is a difference between being included and achieving a sense of belonging, and affinity groups can provide some comfort in fostering a sense of belonging. Having focused his M.Ed. thesis on affinity groups for teachers in independent schools, he strongly advocates for them, especially in the aftermath of the George Floyd murder, the COVID pandemic, and the rise in hate speech and crime toward marginalized groups. Jeannoute notes, "Over the past year [2020–21], Black faculty have alluded to an absence of support during this historic time of racial reckoning."[3]

It is important that affinity groups exist alongside other meaningful practices that form connections among all members of the school community. Our nation's Great Experiment is a work in progress, moving too slowly in ensuring rights, respect, and rewards to many of our fellow citizens. Our schools, too, must play an active role in guiding students toward a more perfect union and the beloved community that Martin Luther King, Jr. envisioned. Respectful, empathetic, and open conversation within the schoolhouse should be within our reach. Our democracy requires no less. There is much work to do.

3. Jeannoute, Bartley. "For the Culture," Master's Thesis, University of Pennsylvania, 2021.

CHAPTER 20

Professional Development
Connecting to the Future

*Can teachers successfully educate children to
think for themselves if teachers are not treated
as professionals who think for themselves?*

Diane Ravitch

To be a teacher intrinsically means to be a learner. Team teaching, all-school themes, adapting curriculum to student interest—all were in essence learning experiences for our teachers throughout the school year. Teachers were always interested in exploring ways to improve practice both with new materials and new approaches, but they were limited by time constraints and responsibilities as a teammate. During the school year, most professional learning was in-house during in-service days or faculty meetings. Many teachers pursued professional development opportunities of their choosing in the summer months, attending a variety of workshops or classes tailored to their own and their students' needs and interests. Several received National Endowment for the Humanities fellowships to take part in one- or two-week workshops. Staying current and innovative in our practice was vital to our pedagogical mission.

LONG-TERM COACHING

One of the most effective in-house development modalities was a multi-year approach to improve writing taught by literacy consultant Susan Radley Brown. Susan used literature as prompts for writing and notebooks to collect ideas. She demonstrated a lesson and her method of conferencing with a student. This was followed by observing and critiquing the teacher. Over several months and several years of return visits, we saw a substantial increase in the quantity of student writing and noticeable improvement in quality.

IN-SERVICE WORKSHOPS

We used in-service days for much of our professional development work. There were at least five days of in-service before the start of the school year, five days at the end of the year, and a few days or half-days interspersed throughout the year. Fall topics were often devoted to preparation for the all-school theme: for example, a presentation by film critic Carrie Rickey on the odyssey theme in films; a day at Shelly Ridge with Leslie Jones Sauer, author of *The Once and Future Forest*; and a workshop with composer Tina Davidson, who guided us in the production of an original percussion and voice interpretation of the myth of Persephone.

In-service work often responded to a current need. We brought in psychiatrist Henry Berger to provide support to faculty and staff after the death of a parent and to discuss how to help children deal with death and grieving. After 9/11, TPS parent Hazami Sayed gave a presentation on Islam, followed by a question-and-answer period; Hazami distributed an extensive list of resources on Islam.

TEAM LEADERS

Another tool for sustaining a learning community was the naming of an administrative team leader for each unit. Their task was to report back to their teaching teams, thereby avoiding using precious all-faculty meeting for administrative tasks. The job of team leader was not one that was envied. Team leaders attended before-school meetings, usually once a month, to review coordination of events, make plans that related to the entire school, or hear announcements about schedule changes.

TEACHER COMMITTEES

Some of our teachers organized themselves into a language arts curriculum committee, and others into a math curriculum group. The language arts curriculum group decided to focus their work on how they used classroom time each week (spelling, grammar, literature, oral and written composition, etc.). They brought their findings to their group, which compared the findings with what was currently described in the school's curriculum, with the Pennsylvania standards for literacy, and with a proposed framework for a revised TPS curriculum. The committee sought to identify what content was missing, underemphasized, or overemphasized. Their findings were brought back to the teaching teams, who reviewed them and then documented what they themselves did in their classrooms and what they hoped to do and why. This was not an argument-free exercise! Disagreements were aired, but the end result was worth the struggle, with faculty better understanding what the students experienced and needed. A similar process was conducted by the math curriculum group.

FACULTY AND STAFF MEETINGS

Our twice-monthly faculty and staff meetings generally began with some general announcements, followed by a sharing session, with each team of teachers sharing a recent highlight from their program. The remainder of the meeting was devoted to a topic meant to get the faculty and staff thinking about new ideas in learning and teaching. It was particularly gratifying to me when a teacher incorporated something I had presented to the group to their own practice. Earlier, I mentioned a presentation that I made on attention to the faculty and staff (a challenge after a long day of teaching). Below is my full lesson, followed by a lesson taught by a middle school teacher to her science classes.

Presentation to faculty on attention. I limited my lesson to 60 minutes. Research on attention suggests that adults can sustain attention for 90 to 110 minutes before they need time to reflect and rest; if the material is complex, then attention can be sustained for less time. I considered this material complex. How better to apply my research on attention than to try to capture the attention of my tired and hungry faculty and staff after a long school day! I tried to model, in the following ways, what I was attempting to teach.

ALERTING FUNCTION. One subsystem of attention is alerting, or preparing to pay attention. Faculty and staff members often came to our after-school meetings exhausted, and the last thing they wanted to do was to muster the energy to attend. I always made sure that food was available and that there was time for friendly conversation before I began the session. Sometimes I determined the seating by teams or by some other variable, depending on the activity, and this also contributes to alerting.

I placed copies of the poem "Once I Looked into Your Eyes" by Paul Muldoon next to the refreshments and wrote an assignment on the board: "Take some food and a copy of the poem to a table. Work with a partner to decipher the poem's meaning. Guess what it means and then return at the end of the talk to see if you have changed your opinion." The title on the board was "Combining Art and Science." Muldoon's poem is below.

> Once I looked into your eyes
> And the only tissue I saw through
> was the tissue of lies
> behind everything you do.
> Once I looked into your heart
> And imagined I could trace
> The history of the art
> Of deception in your face.
> Now there's something more than a chance
> Of making molecules dance
> I'm somewhat gratified to find
> That by laser-enhanced magnetic resonance,
> If nothing else, I may read your mind.

In the past the poet could detect deception by his lover by look-ing into her eyes, but with the advent of functional resonance imagery (fMRI)[1] he does not have to guess—he can read her mind. Not exactly true, but it was the basis for a discussion about fMRI and what increased blood supply to a region of the brain indicates. Faculty and staff also received, in addition to the poem, color copies of the regions of the brain indicating the five lobes and another print showing which regions of the brain are involved in what functions. I also distributed an outline of the talk I would be giving. Entitled "Learning Is the Making of Memories: Without Attention There Is No Memory," the talk included the following topics: gross brain anatomy, definitions of attention, what is attended, factors that influence attention for learning, and the definition and characteristics of the atten-tional network system (alerting, orienting, bottle neck, execu-tive control, or conflict monitoring). During my short lecture, I demonstrated aspects of attention that I was discussing without pointing out immediately what I was doing.

ORIENTING FUNCTION AND BOTTLENECK. Orienting is the per-ceptual aspect of attention (visual, auditory, kinesthetic, or tac-tile) and involves cuing, pointing out what needs to be attended. For example, on concentrating on the subject of alerting, I circu-lated a plastic model of the brain that when opened showed the lobes, which were removable, and the gross anatomy of the inte-rior of the brain when the lobes were removed. As I began speak-ing, alongside a PowerPoint projection that tracked the outline distributed to the staff, I handed the model brain to a teacher and asked him to explore it by removing and then re-assembling the parts and to then pass around the completed brain to the next person. After the model had gone around the room for a few minutes, I asked everyone to recall whether they had been able to examine the model and attend to my voice, the outline,

1. Functional magnetic resonance imaging is the most common type of brain imaging, lighting up parts of the brain while patients think or perform activities.

and the PowerPoint simultaneously? This was a powerful demonstration because almost everyone said that when they had the model in their hands, my voice was in the background and they were not looking at the PowerPoint nor my outline. As we discussed later, this was an example of one of the characteristics of the attentional system—only one thing at a time can be processed, and attended stimuli are given preferential access through what is known to neuroscientists as a "bottleneck."

To demonstrate what does get attended to, I arranged for the building manager and the business manager to have an argument outside an open door while I continued to talk. As the argument grew more heated, one teacher asked if she could shut the door. This occurred, as luck would have it, exactly when I put on the screen a reference to the principle that people automatically attend to abrupt onset of auditory or visual stimuli, especially if the onset is intense, unexpected, or novel. When it happened with such perfect timing, I began to laugh. The audience still did not connect what was occurring with the point I was trying to make. I finally said, "What did you notice about your attention just now?" One teacher said, "It was amazing that the folks outside the room began to argue when you put up that slide and my attention was drawn to the voices. That was really a lucky coincidence." I explained that we had staged the dispute, and most people were surprised.

While I explained the power of salient stimuli, I walked around the room. Individuals would attend better if I spoke close to them; I seemed to be connecting more directly with the people closest to me. (For children, at least, this works because they feel that the teacher is more closely monitoring what they are doing.) As I moved, teachers and staff shifted their position to face me, mainly because they were trying to be polite. But the mere shift of position also helped keep them alert.

EXECUTIVE FUNCTION. Executive control is the ability to monitor attention and to make decisions about changing the focus of attention and planning procedures or processes. When teachers and staff were trying to attend to the lecture, they had to deliberately ignore the staged dispute happening outside of the meeting. They also had to decide whether to listen or to put the parts of the brain model together. I ended the lesson with a quote about executive function for them to ponder. "The effort of attention is a moral act."[2] Mindful, or deliberatively selective, attention can be as strong as novelty, relevance, or cuing.

During the following week, many teachers asked me questions about my lesson or commented on its relevance for them. Later, when I observed teachers in class, we used some of the attentional vocabulary discussed in the lesson. Teachers were more aware of how to get the students ready to attend and how to use novelty and other means to induce orienting. They were also more aware of distractions.

Classroom implementation. I was especially pleased when Laura Matheny, a middle school science teacher who had spent several summers as a brain research assistant at Rockefeller Institute, volunteered to experiment with aspects of attention. She taught science to two relatively heterogeneous groups that met for 80 minutes twice weekly. Each group consisted of approximately 14 vertically grouped sixth, seventh, and eighth graders and the groups were similar in the aptitude spread. The classes were beginning a unit on environmental science, with a study of the volume and characteristics of trash being generated. The goal was to raise student awareness of the kinds and quantities of trash they generated each week. This set the stage for individual projects that were community action oriented and included school and home as well as the wider community. The projects were shown at a science fair for all students and for families of middle school students.

Using one variation of the lesson for an experimental group and another for a control group seemed like a good way to test the effects of some of the factors that influenced the attentional

2. Jeffrey M. Schwartz, M.D. and Sharon Begley, *The Mind and The Brain* (New York: Harper, 2002).

system. The content of the lesson for each group was the same, but the style of teaching varied. The control group received instruction that consisted of good practices but did not include the variables of focused attention tactics. Several days after the lesson we gave the students a quiz to see which group remembered the most.

THE EXPERIMENTAL GROUP. When the students arrived in the class, they noticed four large trash bags sitting in plastic milk crates. The afternoon before, their teacher had collected and saved the day's trash, consisting mainly of partially eaten lunches from the three large middle school trash cans. The trash smelled a little, and the students complained of the odor. Their teacher showed them four large empty milk bins labeled paper, plastic, food, and other. She asked the students, "If you were to separate this trash into these categories, which one would weigh the most?" They predicted paper, followed by plastic, then food, and finally other.

The teacher handed out disposable gloves to the students, and the students gasped. She wasn't really going to ask them to separate the trash, was she? They looked horrified as they waited for the inevitable request. The teacher gave a bag of trash to four groups of four students (the teacher had decided who would be in each group prior to the lesson) and asked them to empty each bag and sort its contents into the proper categories—food, paper, plastic, and other. The students reluctantly stuck their gloved hands into the trash and, groaning and using some mild expletives of disgust, sorted it. After a few minutes, they seemed to overcome their revulsion and began to work with vigor, commenting on the amount of food thrown away, the nature of the food, the paper that should have been recycled, and the unexpected belt and other strange objects that had been discarded. Although they did not admit it, they had a good deal of fun. (One boy, however, looked like he was going to faint, and a few others walked over to the window for fresh air. The lightheaded boy was permitted to watch from a few feet away.)

An informal discussion began in the group about what it

must be like to be a sanitation worker, especially in the summer, and they decided that they were going to investigate what their salaries were and if they received benefits. Their teacher and I reminded them that our own facilities crew and cleaning company faced similar challenges every day. Once the students completed the separation, they took off their gloves, threw them in the "other" category, and ran to wash their hands.

The next set of directions was handed to each individual child even though they were still working in groups. Each redistributed bag of trash was weighed by the teacher, and the weight was recorded on the whiteboard. Each group was assigned one of the redistributed categories (food, paper, plastic, and other). Since they were weighed with the containers, the group had to subtract the weight of the container, which they had determined previously, from the category they were working with.

The assignment was to estimate how much trash the middle school produced each day, then how much the school produced, and then the combined total for the city's 50 independent and charter schools. They also estimated trash production per week. Each group recorded its results on the board. Contrary to their prediction, the students found that more food was wasted than any other category; paper was next, followed by plastic, and then by "other." They estimated that each week the city's independent and charter schools threw out 5,000 pounds of food, 1,000 pounds of paper, 600 pounds of plastic, and 500 pounds of "other."

Asked for their reaction to these numbers, students came up with good reasons for challenging the estimates, which had been extrapolated solely from middle school trash. For example, from their prior experience as "lunch helpers" in the lower grades, they believed that younger children brought big lunches and threw most of them away. In the end, the students decided to accept the percentages observed for each category of trash but agreed that the total amounts could vary. They were horrified by the amount of paper that could have been recycled and by the quantity of food (sandwiches, fruit, and vegetables) that had been wasted. One student said, "That's enough food to feed an entire village!" At this point they discussed bulk as a problem, even though plastic, the bulkiest, weighed less than the food. One seventh grader asked in an exasperated voice, "Are we going to do something about this, or are we going to just talk?"

THE CONTROL GROUP. The control group of students entered the science room the next day, and, so relieved that they did not have to sort trash, immediately sat in their seats alerted to the task at hand. Laura did not have anything on the board to alert them to expectations, but gossip had done that for her. She distributed copies of the workbook *Waste Reduction* (published by Dale Seymour in 1998). The section "Investigate Solid Waste" included a page of discussion questions about the definition of solid waste, how much is thrown away in a typical week, and vocabulary words related to the topic. A second page had a picture of a trash can with percentages of categories that are thrown away. The students answered a few questions with a partner and continued to a third page, which showed a graph of household waste in various countries. With a partner they answered questions and then there was a whole group discussion about their answers. This lesson went on in a similar vein for about 75 minutes, the same amount of time that the experimental group used. Laura did not move around the class as she had in the first group but stayed at the board recording responses. The discussion was lively, but not as detailed as the experimental group in responses or questions. The students also did not ask about actions they could take to improve waste reduction and management.

SUMMARY OF TYPES OF RESPONSES ON THE FACTUAL AND ATTENTION QUESTIONS. The experimental group discussed their results but had no reading material other than homework for the next night comparing Greenland's trash problem to that of the United States. The control group had reading material as well as two visuals, a graph comparing industrialized countries and, again, the picture of the trash with percentages of types of trash.

Both groups were given a two-part quiz three days after their initial experience: the first part related to the content and concepts in the class, and the second part asked about the quality of their attention.

Question	Experimental Group	Control Group
What kind of trash do we generate during the school day?	13 correct and 2 listed items rather than categories	6 correct 8 incorrect
What can be recycled?	13 correct, 1 omitted plastic, most students listed types of plastic and how to distinguish one from the other by the markings	8 correct, 6 only listed paper and no one referred to types of plastic
What stands out for you?	Answers were more detailed and creative and included good conversation, we could express our opinion, Laura talked to us, worry about landfill space, how they felt about the sanitation workers, how much we use, how wasteful we are, education is needed, it was a cool lesson	The basic response here was the US uses too much and has the most trash. This was based on the graph in the reading material.
Was it easy or difficult to attend to the lesson? Why?	All but two students said it was easy and fun. The two that said it was difficult said it was too disgusting, while their responses to the questions indicated that they were attending but as they said, "grossed out."	7 said it was easy to attend and 7 said it was difficult. Comments like "boring," "I had to take notes to pay attention," "I couldn't visualize anything" were very common. One student said, "you, Laura, made it very easy."

Laura and I had used two attention variables, alerting and novelty, in the experimental group. During that group lesson, Laura had employed alerting by circulating from group to group, asking questions, and keeping the task at hand salient. A comment from a student indicated that she felt as if Laura was directly talking to her group and that made it easy for her to pay attention. When Laura stood in front of the class, she and I noticed less grappling with the subject, almost a total lack of emotional engagement. The fact that the teacher was circulating, showing her own interest, made a difference.

The novelty in the experimental group's lesson was also key to fostering student engagement. In his book *Surprise, Uncertainty, and Mental Structures* (2002), psychologist Jerome Kagan referred to numerous studies suggesting that humans seek novelty and that novelty will almost always capture attentional resources from each of the three subsystems of attention (alerting, orientation, and executive control). However, individuals become easily habituated to what was initially novel; the effects of introducing something novel are temporary. Kagan also stated that the novelty cannot be totally out of the norm, which is dependent on the developmental age. He explained that young children fear clowns because they are human but nothing about them is recognizable; a young child does not have schema for clown.

The trash as novelty involved familiar material, and the students guessed that they were not going to find anything horribly repellent. The activity engaged them both on an intellectual as well as on an emotional level. Hands-on learning was so much a part of our school culture that the experiment piece was not novel but what we used as material to engage was. Compared to the control group, the experimental group remembered more and was eager to continue to explore the problem of solid waste.

A fascinating aspect of this experiment was that the students in the control group who found that the workbook kept their attention were students who tend to process information more slowly than the others. And one of the two students in the experimental group who found it difficult to attend because the material was "nasty" was also a slow processor; this activity had required multi-tasking and multiple perspectives, whereas the tasks of the control group had been linear.

Laura and I shared the experiment and results with the faculty. The results raised questions about teacher practice, experiential learning, and differentiated instruction since what was good for some students was not for others. We saw the importance of putting attention central in lesson design and understanding the variables that impact the ability to stay on task. Teachers recognized the power of asking students to examine their own ability to attend, thereby increasing their own awareness of what it meant to pay attention. With so many so-called "brain-based" educational materials on the market, I hoped this work would help make the faculty more sophisticated and discerning about their merits.

COLLABORATIVE INQUIRY GROUPS

In 2005, I experimented with creating a different kind of faculty leadership. I organized a "collaborative inquiry group" (CIG), consisting of at least one teacher from each of our teaching teams (each participating teacher received extra compensation), the school's learning specialist, the co-principal, and me. Its mission was to focus on selected learning situations that teachers brought to the group from their own teaching teams. After studying the chosen issue as a group, CIG teachers took their findings back to their teaching teams for further analysis and exchange of views. This was followed by a full-faculty discussion about the topic. The theory was that the CIG teachers would function as catalysts for learning within their teams.

At our first CIG meeting, held after student dismissal, we decided to meet bi-weekly, to rotate leadership, and to study areas of interest in depth. We also agreed that trust within the group was important; the teachers wanted to bring up difficulties in an honest way, not just talk about how well their work was going. There were questions about comfort with administrators being present; I said I hoped that the group would not feel judged and that perhaps we could add to the discussion or help solve problems.

Susan Bodley, a Primary Unit teacher, was our facilitator. At our first meeting we chose questions to consider throughout the year, always bringing evidence from our classrooms: What kind of interactions foster active learning? How do we know that students are learning? Do teachers talk too much? How do we build inquiry into all subjects? How do we structure student groups for discussion?

One of the topics explored by CIG was constructivism in mathematics. The CIG teachers asked their teaching teams to present two complex mathematics problems to their math groups: one would be presented in a constructivist manner, and the other in a conventional manner. The CIG members brought back to the study group evidence as to how the teachers in their respective teams felt the lessons were effective and how much time each lesson required (time being one of the issues for constructivist learning). The practical issue for exploration was whether to present the algorithm first or at any point before the end of the lesson or only after students explored fully various solutions. The conclusion was that the latter led to more lasting understanding and skill.

JAPANESE LESSON STUDY

Prior to the opening of school in September 2004, teachers attended an all-day presentation by Columbia University Professor Barbrina Ertle on Japanese lesson study, a professional development tool designed and used in Japan that enables teachers to systematically and collaboratively conduct research on teaching and learning internally, in their own classrooms. It is a process for creating deep and grounded reflection about the complex activities of teaching that can be shared and discussed with other members of the profession.

The faculty had for several years been talking about the need to observe each other to improve practice. Most of our continual improvements focused on curricula rather than practice, believing that team teaching provided enough observation to help each other internalize good practice and discard what did not work. Observations were primarily within the team, and the process was informal. In addition, every team member valued teaching time and was reluctant to leave their own students with their teammates, thereby placing an added burden on them.

One of our middle school teachers, Chris Taranta, had returned from a one-year Klingenstein fellowship at Columbia University's Teachers' College, where he had been introduced to Japanese lesson study. At the time, I was looking for a research project for my doctoral program at Penn's Graduate School of Education. When Chris described Japanese lesson study to me, I felt it met all the criteria of what the faculty was looking for, with the added benefit of my own research to help us evaluate whether lesson study made a difference in practice and, ultimately, in student learning. Of course, always aware that when something is added, something must go, we made participation in the study voluntary. Chris and I presented the plan to the faculty, hoping that some teachers would sign on to try the multi-month practice, which consisted of eight steps: defining the overarching goals, planning the research lesson, teaching the lesson, evaluating the lesson, revising the lesson, teaching the revised lesson, evaluating the revised lesson, and sharing the results in a written report.[3]

Middle School teachers applied lesson study to a lesson on Chaucer's *Canterbury Tales*, a 14th-century account of a group of pilgrims competing in a story-telling contest as they traveled from London to a shrine in Canterbury. After reading the *Tales*, students were assigned the role of one of the characters and asked to select a congenial traveling companion from among the other characters in the group. Here are reflections afterwards from two Middle School teachers:

3. J. W. Stigler & J. Hiebert (1999). *The Teaching Gap: Best Ideas from the World's Teachers for Improving in the Classroom* (New York: The Free Press, 1999).

In our lesson, each student was asked to decide which
other character would make a good traveling companion for the character whose role that student was playing.
I was concerned that students might ask other students
questions based on 21st century criteria, rather than criteria from the tales. This sort of thing happens all the time
in Middle School, peer concerns overriding the lesson on
the characters. The overarching goal of community and
character brought an important lens to our study.

In planning the lesson, many times a comment from
one person triggered an idea from another and suddenly
there was insight about a practice or a child. When discussing how to introduce *Canterbury Tales* to students
with varying reading levels, one teacher suggested a
practice such as taking notes and another teacher suggested giving the students a chart for their responses that
would help the slower processors. These small changes
were very effective.

An observing teacher from the Junior Unit provided the following feedback, after which the lesson was revised and improved:

As an observer of this *Canterbury* lesson, I heard students use criteria that were in fact based on their character roles. One student said to another, "We should
be together, we both like hunting." These two students
were not friends but were able to evaluate social criteria.
Another said to a friend who was also the Wife of Bath,
"I can't go with you, you are married, and I am a monk!"

Japanese lesson study was tried by several teaching teams,
some using the approach's strict protocols and others a modi-
fied version of the protocols. As the comments below show, there
were mixed reactions to our exploration of lesson study.

"If we try to keep [its overarching goals] in front of us, that
will change things." (Junior Unit teacher).

"When you go as an observer in someone else's classroom that, too, benefits the overarching goals because you're finding out more about community." (Primary Unit teacher)

"Peer observation makes people feel more a part of the community. Lines between units are not drawn as thickly. Once you do it there are lots of benefits, especially in terms of the cross units." (Kindergarten teacher)

"We are imagining all of the possibilities when you build the lesson, and then you get to actually see what happens when you enter the kids into it, which is always a piece of the puzzle that you don't know about. We were really just interested to see what would happen as the people that came to observe." (Middle School teacher).

"We are constantly evaluating whether we're doing what's best for kids and the class, teaching in the best way and learning the most. You learn from peers as these questions arise." (Kindergarten teacher)

"It wasn't a personal kind of thing; you were focused on the lesson itself and then how kids fit into that." (Junior Unit teacher)

"Observing was very cool. It's always cool to watch what somebody's doing, and you get ideas, or you learn from their mistakes and from their successes." (Middle School teacher)

"We felt the protocol was too rigid and didn't fit us, our school, or our department." (Art teacher)

"There was a certain amount of artificiality that felt inherent to the lesson study process. I think the whole process could be kept simpler." (Spanish teacher)

"We were able to pick it (protocol) apart, what do we like about this. Let's try to continue that and figure out how much structure is needed to keep it positive and exciting for each of us." (Middle School teacher).

"It can be intimidating." (Kindergarten teacher)

"I was very nervous, and I felt that the process was nerve-wracking. I was very apprehensive about it happening and

> then when it happened, I was stiffer and not myself. . . . I
> have been a teacher for fifteen years and then all of a sud-
> den, I'm a wreck. It was like taking an exam when you
> hadn't taken an exam in forever." (Art teacher)

"I was concerned about losing the respect of my peers."
(Spanish teacher)

Overall, the teachers were good sports about trying this bur-
densome practice. We concluded that we would like to continue
to practice some type of peer observation. However, there were
several reasons why lesson study might work in Japan but not in
the United States. Two of the main ones were that teachers in
Japan can leave their students unsupervised, not needing to find
someone to cover their classes, and that they are given far more
time to pursue the observations.

The final report of a 12-member "stakeholders group" was
that they agreed with the central purposes of lesson study: (1)
to create a culture of reflection in which teachers as researchers
look at practice and its effect on student learning and (2) more
importantly, to create a professional community that is comfortable saying, "I am not certain how to do this. Can you help me?
Can we try to figure this out together?" The recommendation
for future action was to develop a system that achieves the benefits of lesson study without the formality and inflexibility of the
Japanese version and utilizes peer observation without undue
focus on the teacher. The stakeholders group proposed a system they called "lesson sharing," which would include looking
at a lesson, reflecting and focusing on student learning through
observations of students and their work.

I regret the discomfort experienced by some of the teachers,
but I am proud that we embarked on a shared experience that
represented a willingness to take risks to advance practice for
the benefit of student learning. I am not sure I heard all of the
grumbling, but I appreciated the honest and open conversations
surrounding the project.

CHAPTER 21

Outcomes

Community involves collaborative activity
whose consequences are appreciated as good
by the individuals who participate. The good
is realized in such a way and shared by so many
that people desire to maintain it.
When this happens, there is community.

Maxine Green, *Releasing the Imagination* (1995)

OUTCOMES. In the world of education, too often the word "outcomes" typically means test scores, high school or college admissions, incomes. For me, it has always been a learning community—faculty and students—whose values, experiences, and actions enable them to respond reflectively and fairly to challenges ahead. A democratic society requires that schools help children learn to cope with uncertainty, learn how to learn for life, and learn to make informed choices and decisions.

Our eighth graders left us after the close of their Graduation Ceremony, which in design was a metaphor for the school's focus on the individual, connections, and community. It was a carefully choreographed event that celebrated each graduating eighth grader and, at the same time, communicated to the assembled guests—parents, grandparents, faculty and staff, trustees, and every single TPS student—the essence of our community of learners.

Closing ceremonies featured individual speeches or musical

performances by each of our graduating students. A rite of passage that even our youngest children knew would one day be theirs, graduation was the culmination of years of speaking up in class, sharing ideas and opinions, asking questions, and performing in plays, musicals, and recitals. And year after year, they themselves had not only attended graduation but also played a role during closing ceremonies—the preschoolers presented flowers to each graduate, the kindergartners sang "Make New Friends" alongside the graduates, and each unit chorus punctuated the program with choral performances. Over the years, many children told me that as early as kindergarten they began to think about what they would say or do on their graduation day.

Preparation for graduation was a month-long process, with two or three periods a week devoted to it. The eighth graders met with me, as well as with two other long-time administrators with experience working with students on writing. Our music teachers worked with the eighth graders to perform a group song, usually rewriting the lyrics to a favorite melody. The students voted on the music for the processional and recessional (played on piano, not "piped in"). Students who chose to sing or perform an instrumental piece in lieu of the song received coaching from a music teacher.

Graduation prep focused on speech writing and delivery (even musical performers needed to present an introduction to their performances). Students learned the difference between essay writing and speech writing. They "brainstormed" possible topics for their speeches, which had a limit of 2 ½ minutes. We wanted them to think deeply about meaningful experiences that had occurred during their years at TPS. They asked themselves, Why was this event meaningful to me? Who was involved? What did I learn from the experience? Why was it so funny or scary?

Once their speeches were written, the students practiced, practiced, and practiced, first in small groups and then at a podium in front of the whole graduating class. (Perhaps unbeknownst to the students, learning how to write and deliver a speech was part of the language arts curriculum!) Attention was then turned to the ceremony, which on graduation day would depend fully on the graduates. As a group, they were responsible for the processional, the order of the speeches and musical performances, the recessional, and other parts of the ceremony. Interdependence and community were the order of the day—it was up to each of them to represent their class. The class worked on sitting up tall and not slouching, the "chair rockers" stopped rocking, the chatterboxes quieted down, and the girls in 2-inch heels stopped wobbling (mostly). We asked the students to use their judgment in terms of what they wore on graduation day; as this was a time when sneakers and jeans were, unlike today, not considered appropriate for "formal occasions," we asked the students not to wear them. We did suggest that students sitting in the front row of the raised platform not wear short skirts that might allow the audience to see their underwear! Individual choice was emphasized with decorum in mind; we were never disappointed.

While the students were prepping for graduation, their middle school teachers were preparing speeches about each of their advisees and thoughtfully choosing a gift for them. You can imagine how moving these good-byes were; most of the teacher-advisee relationships were over the course of three years. Very frequently a teacher's speech about an advisee unknowingly echoed remarks of the student's speech; it was powerful when this happened.

Gifts to advisees were as varied as the recipients. An avid writer might receive a journal; a reader, a book that reflected the advisor's or the child's interests. One student who always wrote his weekly journal entries in poetic form to his advisor, Judith Parker, received a pocket-sized *Oxford Book of English Verse* that she found in a secondhand bookstore.

A particularly emotional moment was when teacher Steve Bartholomew took a copper bracelet off his own wrist and gave it to his advisee. The bracelet had been given to Steve as a gift to "protect him," and he always wore it. Steve explained to his advisee, who had sometimes struggled with life at school, that he was giving him the bracelet to acknowledge how he had overcome challenges and to remind him of his advisor's confidence in him. Some advisors went to considerable lengths to find a meaningful gift. Judith enrolled in a ceramics class to learn how to make tiles so she could create one for an advisee. The tile re-created the cover of the program for *A Midsummer Night's Dream*; the original cover art, depicting Titania, had been created by the advisee, who played Titania in the play.

On the morning of graduation, I met with the students to talk to them about choices they would be facing during the years ahead. It was always challenging to launch these graduates, most of whom had been with us for nine years in a relatively protected environment, a place where they were known and cared for, into the larger world of high school, with all the temptations, choices, and adventures that lay ahead. Since each student was probably nervous about the challenges of graduation day, it was unlikely that they heard my message.

As soon as the first notes of processional played, the eighth graders began their Graduation Ceremony, admittedly with several of the girls still teetering onto the stage in their dramatically high heels. I sat in the front row to prompt and cue, but that was rarely necessary. A simple nod to show my confidence was sufficient for each student as they reached the podium. Speech topics were always delightfully varied: for example, "Ode to My Smiling Teachers," "Felt with the Heart," "Yo, Muse," "Questions Left Unanswered," "Laughing at TPS," "A Midsummer Night's Dream," and "Batter Up." The assembled guests learned something about each student, but the speeches collectively formed a series of vignettes that painted a picture of life at TPS. Sometimes a single speech said it all. Callie Lefevre '01 read her poem "Nothing Would I Change," describing her visit to a suburban high school she was considering attending.

"Hello!" I called out, when I saw my guide.
"You must be Callie!" she kindly replied.

"What school d'you go to?" she asked, sounding cool.
I smiled and said, "The Philadelphia School."
"Well yeah, I know that, but what is it called?"
"Oh no, that's the name." I muttered appalled.
    "So, let's go to class, history is next."
"Great, I love Theme!" She looked at me vexed.
"History, you know, like wars and dominions."
    "No, Theme, I said, "ideas and opinions."
    "History, cultures and artifacts found."
"No, Theme, Olympics, Time, Underground
We write Theme reports, like long dissertations
On War and Peace or Catilinarian Orations."
    "Whatever, at least, I hope I may say
    That science is next, we've got lab today."
"Science class on Tuesday? Really, how droll.
I forgot you spend all week inside school.
We go to Shelly Ridge and learn from nature,
We cut away vines and help plants mature."
"Gard'ning? You're kidding. Did you get an A?"
"We don't get grades. It's not the TPS way."
"But how do you know if your work is strong?"
"Well, we get "checks" as we're going along.
Check minus is bad, check plus is real fine—
Check plus plus is great, I get one sometimes,
    If Emily or Steve is feeling nice,
You might get check plus smiley face for spice."
"Emily and Steve? Where're are the misses and misters?
You refer to your teachers like brothers and sisters."
"You mean family groups with Thanksgiving feasts,
Only with school baked lasagna and celery treats.?"
    "Thanksgiving in a lunchroom? That's a whim."
    "No, there's no lunchroom, we eat in the gym.
We don't have desks either, or lockers and things.
We hardly have walls, or class bells that ring."
    "I've heard that about inner-city schools—
How they don't have theaters or swimming pools.

> I'm sure you're glad to be moving on
> To playing fields, and a school with a lawn."
> "Taney's our lawn, the city's our field.
> It's the odd things that have such appeal.
> Wherever I go, a TPSer I'll stay.
> If I didn't have to leave, I'd never go away."
> My guide stared at me as I fought back the tears.
> Memories came flooding from all my eight years.
> This school is my childhood, to some it is strange,
> To me it is home, there's nothing I would change.

After every five or six speeches, a song was performed in the students' honor by one of the school's choruses. Facing the graduates, the children, led by our chorus director, sang pieces that they had prepared throughout the spring for this occasion. In 2006 the Primary Unit sang *May You Always Have a Song* (by Sally K. Albrecht and Jay Althouse); the Junior Unit, *This Shall Be for Music* (poem by Robert Louis Stevenson, music by Mark Patterson); and Middle School, *Ain't No Mountain High Enough* (by Nick Ashford and Valerie Simpson). For the sixth and seventh graders, this was the first time they had sung as a chorus without the eighth grade. Many sang with tears streaming down their faces. They had good friends among the graduates, having learned and played together throughout their time at TPS.

Each graduation featured a guest speaker. As varied as our graduates, they included TPS graduate Dr. Sarah Dry '87 (writer and historian); sculptor and author Anne Truitt; beloved TPS kindergarten teacher Anne Greenwald; Philadelphia Mayor Ed Rendell (later governor); NASA astronaut Jeffrey Hoffman (who on his fourth mission repaired the Hubble Space Telescope); TPS parent Reverend Willett A. Burgie; president of the TPS Board of Trustees, Robert Adelson; president of University Science Center, Dr. Randall M. Whaley; astronomer Derrick Pitts; Congressman Peter Kostmayer; and Superintendent of Schools for Harlem Children's Zone, Dr. Doreen Land.

Here are some of their memorable messages to our graduating eighth graders.

Sarah Dry, June 1999: "For me, this necessary uncertainty boils down to one thing: take confidence in who you are right now and don't wait to become something else. It takes a while to get used to the fact that you are who you are. The scenery changes, and you live and learn, but your essential 'youness' stays with you. An ancient Greek philosopher named Heraclitus famously proclaimed that we never step into the same river twice. What I'd like to add is that no matter how different the river, wherever we go, there we are, as we are, as we have been. We carry our history with us. . . . I've always felt most truly myself, when I was actively learning and testing myself, when I felt challenged by the world around me. . . . I encourage you to seek these challenges out. Don't wait for them to find you."

Anne Truitt, June 1997: "When we are young, as you are, we dream dreams—and in dreams begin responsibilities. We make promises to ourselves. These promises are first imaginary. We imagine what we might like to become— a poet, a teacher, a doctor, a lawyer, a mother or a father, a space explorer, a scientist. You promise yourself more personal things too, that you will try to be a kind person, for example, someone who tries to understand other people. Gradually, the promises that you make to yourself turn into goals toward which you can work intelligently. You begin to train yourself to make your dreams come true."

Rev. Willette A. Burgie, 2002: "You want to know something really scary??? The seeds of terrorism lie in the hearts and minds and spirits of each and every one of us. Seeds of hatred and of desecration, seeds of destructive willfulness, violence, self-aggrandizement, and irreverence. But

thanks be to God, those are not the only seeds we all har-
bor. Inside of each of us there are also the seeds of love and
of compassion, seeds of dignity and nobility, of peace and
of peace-making. Seeds of kindness, generosity and ten-
derness, seeds of courage and of hope and of great, great
faith-all of that, inside each of us. . . . I want to leave you
with a question: which seeds will you choose? Moment
to moment, for the rest of your lives, you get to choose
which seeds will find life in you, which seeds will gain life
through you."

Anne Greenwald, 2000: "I'm especially pleased to be participating in this moment of transition from TPS to the rest
of your lives. It is particularly meaningful to me because
I remember another moment of transition. When each of
you arrived at The Philadelphia School.

A small picture . . . Will I ever forget that all Anna
wanted for her sixth birthday was a yellow bikini? Of
course, I do have the yellow bikini Bic to remind me."

[Anne continues to paint a picture with words of a
moment she remembers for each member of the class of
2000, even those who did not begin in TPS kindergarten.]

"The world is always telling us to look at the large picture, step back and see the whole but often from my perspective it is the small pictures rather than the large one
that leave a child indelibly printed in my mind. Put enough
of the small pictures together and you will begin to get the
larger picture of a child, adult or even a situation.

". . . But as each of you goes off to your new school,
remember to stay focused on one picture at a time, don't
be in too much of a hurry to make a big judgment, until
you have a firm sense of all the small pictures and what
you can learn from each of them as they gather to make a
portfolio of new friends and experiences, once you have
that portfolio you'll be ready to do whatever your little
hearts desire."

Doreen Land, 2006: ". . . I chose the road less traveled. This road was filled with pebbles, the pebbles of pain, abandonment, disappointment, and loneliness. The road was long and arduous. The reward came in the realization that I was the architect of my life, the person responsible for my dreams, and future. This ignited a fire within me that reaches new heights every day. . . . Continue to fuel the fire of learning which you began at TPS. Ignite the miracle that you are for it is this fire that will bring you peace and happiness and the ability to ignite the fires for those that will follow. Just remember, as you begin your transition into high school, that you alone can make a difference in this world. I too sat where you are today; I had fears and insecurities that sometimes stifled my ability to make decisions. But, regardless of these fears, I succeeded and so will you; just as the focus of your theme study this year, Benjamin Franklin, demonstrated throughout his life that one man can make an everlasting impact upon the world. The challenge awaits you. . . ."

Once speeches and performances were completed, the eighth graders sang their class song; in 2006 the song was *Our Lives* by Aaron Kamin and Alex Band. It was then my turn to address the graduates. Here is an excerpt from my final speech as head of The Philadelphia School in June 2006.

Today, as at every graduation, we experience the joy that comes with knowing our young people are ready for the next step and the sadness that accompanies letting go. . . . I would like to return to images from E.B. White's tale *Charlotte's Web* to describe what may be experienced today by TPS faculty and staff, parents, guardians, and grandparents, on one hand, and graduates on the other.

In the last chapter, after Charlotte the spider has died and her babies have emerged from their sacs, Wilbur the pig was cheered up by the idea that he will be surrounded by Charlotte's children. Then, the farmer opened the barn door bringing in a warm breeze. And the baby spiders felt and responded to the warm updraft.

"One spider climbed to the top of the fence and did something that came as a great surprise to Wilbur. The spider stood on its head, pointed its spinnerets in the air, and let loose a cloud of fine silk. The silk formed a balloon. As Wilbur watched, the spider let go of the fence and rose in the air. 'Goodbye!' it said, as it sailed through the doorway. 'Wait a minute!' screamed Wilbur. 'Where do you think you're going?'" One after another, the spiders sailed away. "'Come back, children!' he cried." One spider stopped to explain: "'This is our moment for setting forth. We are aeronauts and we are going out into the world to make webs for ourselves.'"

In that spirit, I wish you, the class of 2006, a beautiful journey; may you spin many clouds of fine silk and, in time, spin beautiful webs. Now is the moment when you become graduates of The Philadelphia School.

I called the name of each graduate, who came forward for a hug. Our admissions director, Abby Levner, who had first met the students when they applied to TPS, shook their hands as they walked toward the president of the Board of Trustees, who congratulated the students as they received their diplomas. As I officially declared them to be graduates, the class formed a line in front of their applauding and cheering audience. The kindergarteners came forward, one or two standing in front of each graduate, and together they sang "Make New Friends." Next came the preschoolers, who presented each graduate with a flower. The graduates then excitedly receded out to the music of their choice and met their families and friends in the school yard.

The remaining students said good-bye to all their teachers, past and present, who stood in a line down the exit staircase and out toward the school yard. This was a bittersweet moment, filled both with sadness at leaving teachers and friends and with joy as they looked forward to summer vacation.

Why am I focusing on one day, Graduation Day, in a chapter entitled "Outcomes"? The day symbolized, year in and year out, what we as educators aimed to impart to our students, day in and day out. Value as an individual. A creative spirit. Connection to a community. Empathy toward others. Active stewardship of the community, the city, and the natural world. An understanding, to repeat the words of the late John Lewis, that "democracy is an act, and each generation must do its part."

I continue to learn that alumni are living lives that reflect our aspirations as educators for them. They include teachers and professors, visual and performing artists, environmentalists, urbanists, computer scientists, doctors, nurses, entrepreneurs, public servants, personal trainers, nonprofit leaders, and even a deejay. Alumni serve on the boards of nonprofits, many are politically active, some coach Little League, and others make community service a priority in their lives. They are creative and curious, and they care.

I would like to think that the interdisciplinary nature of our program—particularly the central role of the arts—was influential in the interesting lives alumni are leading. We have a ballet instructor who is an activist against fast fashion, shopkeepers who design the latest hip-hop fashions, a software engineering manager who is also a recording artist, a communications specialist who combined his love of basketball and his academic training to work in the front office of an NBA team, and a nurse who plays bass in a band.

It is also gratifying for me to know that there are alumni whose professional work centers on the environment. These include a marine biologist who combines science and advocacy to help restore the health of the Delaware River watershed; a capital projects administrator who works for the NYC Department of Environmental Protection; an environmental archaeologist who studies the long-term sustainability of agriculture and land use; and a natural resources biologist who manages wetlands and stream restoration projects in Maryland.

Over the years I have received letters and emails from alumni who shared with me the impact a TPS education had on their lives and work. I include three below.

Sarah Dry '87 in 2003 (author of *Curie*, *The Newton Papers: The Strange and True Odyssey of Isaac Newton's Manuscripts*, and *Waters of the World*):

> I've recently rediscovered the joys of education. After working briefly in the exciting world of biotechnology in southern California, I realized that I was really interested in studying science rather than helping to do it. I recently finished a master's in history of science, technology, and medicine at Imperial College in London, and I've just started my first year of a PhD in History of Science at Cambridge University. I'm looking at 19th-century railway accidents in Britain and trying to do both a social and scientific history of risk. This is fun because I get to look at all kinds of documents, from bureaucratic government reports to sensational newspaper stories and scientific journals. . . . I am happy to be a student again. It's almost as good as TPS days, making leaf identification booklets and learning the queen Mab speech for *Romeo and Juliet*.

Ben West '93 in 2006 (currently Assistant Federal Public Defender, District of New Jersey):

> Working now, as I do, in indigent criminal defense, I spend a lot of time in federal prison. The environment of the prison is as far from the open, curious, utopian, family community I enjoyed at TPS as any place I can imagine. In prison nothing seems possible. The emphasis seems to be on denying the prisoners their own sense of self-worth and dignity. I feel one of my primary respon-

sibilities is to return that dignity to my clients, to open new possibilities to them, and to help them believe in their own future.

TPS showed me what becomes possible when a community sets the right priorities. With all the empty talk of values this year, I am especially grateful for the example of TPS. It was there that I came to deeply believe in my own ability to effect change in the world. I bring TPS with me into the prisons and federal court, and I try to share it with my clients.

If I am grounded in anything, it is in The Philadelphia School. Thank you for creating an institution that has inspired me and that I carry with me as a model for the good that can be achieved in this world."

Gabriel Tames '93 in 2006 (currently attorney, Court of Appeal, Third District, CA):

My 9 years at TPS provided a wonderful foundation for my studies in higher education. I have no doubt that TPS's pedagogical commitment to interdisciplinarily "engaging" with the object of inquiry (whether staging a production of *Romeo and Juliet* in conjunction with reading the play in language arts class, creating a glazed clay Grecian urn in art class while studying ancient Greece in theme class, or role playing predators and preys in the forest of Shelley Ridge while learning the complexities and interdependence of the food chain in science class) continues to be a driving force in my approach to life and learning today.

Throughout college and law school I found that I am most excited (and most successful) when my courses connect to each other and the world I am experiencing. In law school, my studies—and my sense of social responsibility—were both strengthened when I taught classes on "searches and seizures," "Miranda" and "attorney-client privilege" at local youth detention centers at the same time that I was taking criminal law classes in the manicured surroundings of Stanford's campus.

Next year I will be clerking at the Supreme Court of New Jersey helping one of the justices interpret the state and federal constitutions and state statutes. The foundation of critical reading and creative thinking that I developed at TPS (upon which I intellectually developed in high school, college, and law school) will undoubtedly serve me well next year and beyond."

CHAPTER 22
_____

Closing Thoughts

If we teach today's students as we taught yesterday's,
we rob them of tomorrow.

John Dewey

DEWEY WROTE the words above in 1916, more than 100 years ago, and sadly his statement is widely disputed as culture wars continue across the nation. Fueled by social media, people's attention is turned to simple explanations for complex issues. We increasingly lack models for debate and patience to consider multiple perspectives. Politicization of COVID-19 mitigation has led to a widespread distrust in science. MAGA extremists have pit "parents' rights" against the professional practice and wisdom of educators. As discussed earlier, politicians and school boards are requiring curricula that ban books, limit teacher speech, and exclude discussion of topics related to race, gender, or anything deemed "unpatriotic." These policies are disingenuous or, to be more generous, baseless efforts to protect the status quo by preventing students from learning to think for themselves.

This trend certainly is a backwards one, and I have no doubt that John Dewey would be appalled by how children are being robbed of the tools that will ensure a future in a healthy democratic society. Only by honestly and freely addressing the issues of the day—and their roots in the past—can students be equipped and empowered to move this nation forward.

Throughout my long career, I had been optimistic that progressive trends in teacher training would result in an American public education system that Dewey envisioned. I had hoped that schools throughout the country would be settings where the complex issues of the day could be openly addressed with reflection, patience, humility, and courage.

The type of learning community we created and sustained at The Philadelphia School was such a setting. And it should not and need not be a rarity. As Aeschylus wrote nearly 2,500 years ago, "Memory is the mother of all wisdom." Today's students should be comparing George Washington's decision to step down from the presidency at the end of his second term to the efforts to prevent the peaceful transfer of power after the 2020 presidential election. They should be discussing the current controversies surrounding the removal of Confederate statues and monuments, as well as memorials to such diverse figures as explorer Christopher Columbus, founding father Thomas Jefferson, and gynecologist J. Marion Sims.

A dynamic educational program such as ours depends fundamentally on an institution that nurtures both the child and the teacher in terms of values, creativity, and intellectual pursuits. Dewey, when asked what the principal aims a school should set for itself to foster the development of educated persons in a democracy, answered, "What the best and wisest parent wants for his own child, that must the community want for all its children. Any other ideal for our schools is narrow and unlovely: acted upon, it destroys our democracy." While just who should be considered the "best and wisest parent" certainly is debatable in a 21st-century context, what Dewey meant at the time was that all children should be provided with the education and social conditions we would choose for our own. With guidance from trusted and trusting adults, children can learn to think critically and make choices that will further democratic life in our nation.

How, in a nutshell, can this be accomplished?

First, there must be respect for children and childhood. At The Philadelphia School we paid close attention to the latest research on child development and tailored content to be developmentally appropriate.

Second, teachers deserve respect. Teachers are professionals and should be treated as such by school administrators, parents, and politicians. We respected the individual teacher and gave teachers the freedom to create and deliver curricula within the parameters of the school philosophy. We recognized that teaching is part art, part skill, and part commitment to producing an educated citizenry.

At the center of creating curricula to educate the intellect and character of our students were questions: What skills and why? What content and why? What is best for the individual child? These questions were debated, using evidence when available and trusting the intuition and experience of the teacher. We shared the belief that the students needed to master skills as tools, not ends in themselves, and to acquire knowledge about the past. We believed that the more one knows and understands, the richer life will be.

We believed in the power of connections, a recurring theme in this book. Through these connections, we modeled democratic values through everyday practices—considering multiple perspectives; practicing self-advocacy; collaborating with others; being responsive to the needs of the school community, the city, and the natural world; and identifying problems and taking action to solve them. All this developed an open-mindedness, a crucial quality that makes legitimate disagreement possible and acceptable.

Learning is life. School should be a place where children develop a passion for learning and take pleasure in meaningful work. At TPS, students were surrounded by teachers who were passionate about their discipline, and they witnessed what it means to be engrossed in and excited by the pursuit of knowledge. Students came to know not only the joy of learning but also how one thought as, for example, a scientist, an artist, or a historian.

Change is a natural aspect of a healthy organization, one that is responsive to changes in society (without succumbing to negative influences like cynicism, lack of civility, and fear), changes in what we knew about teaching and learning, and changes in our students. Our future depends on departing from the past. Yet there is an inherent, contradictory tension in making change. This tension is healthy in that it tempers our decision-making. In terms of an education program, we make choices regarding skills versus content, historical versus contemporary content, cooperation versus competition, individual potential versus teamwork, freedom versus responsibility, and social moral conventions versus autonomy.

Each of us changes as we learn and experience more. Some changes at TPS were minor, for example, changing the structure of student learning groups. Others were fundamental, such as increasing the school's enrollment and, by teacher request, lengthening the school day. Some changes involved taking risks to try to improve student outcomes, for example, our experiment with Japanese Lesson Study. What did not change was maintaining intellectual rigor.

Nor did we change our emphasis on the individual child and what was best for that child. As a small school—in my last year as head with an enrollment of 371 and a student-teacher ratio of 12:1—we were able to know each child well. We avoided undue standardization; one size did not fit all in terms of content delivery, assessment, and discipline. We helped students identify their strengths and provided opportunities for them to share their talents with the community. Everyone had something to contribute to our community.

But a small-school model is not all that matters. A principal or head of school needs to be, first and foremost, an educational leader. A head of school must have frequent direct contact with the faculty, the students, and the families. I was in classrooms every day, I took part in curriculum study groups, I attended Spanish class with students for several years, and I taught mini-courses. Bureaucracy can be successfully limited through distributed leadership, with staff and teachers sharing the responsibilities of keeping the school running efficiently. Imposing a corporate business model might work in the school's finance office but not in the classroom.

Was everything perfect? Of course, not. In 1787, our nation's founders gathered in Philadelphia and set forth the aspiration to create a "more perfect union." Two centuries later, in our small corner of that city, we educators likewise strove to improve our practice so that students were empowered to see themselves as makers of change—citizens prepared to confront issues large and small.

In spring 2007, I closed my final Annual Report to the school community with these words:

> It has been a privilege to head The Philadelphia School for the past 23 years. I have loved my work, my colleagues, the students, and the parents. I have appreciated your support and trust; you gave me the courage and encouragement to act on a vision. TPS has been everything I dreamed of when I thought about what I wanted to promote in my professional life for the benefit of children: use of the city, environmental study, interdisciplinary work, thematic and experiential education, teacher study groups, teacher autonomy, and the freedom to experiment.

> We were part of A Great Experiment.

Acknowledgments

Piglet noticed that even though he had a Very Small Heart,
it could hold a rather large amount of Gratitude.

A.A. Milne

FIRST AND FOREMOST, I am grateful to the founders of The Philadelphia School, Caroline Simon and Lynne Berman. Fifty years ago, supported by their husbands, Richard Laden and Peter Berman, they established their ideal school, grounded in progressive educational philosophy and practice. Their school—which they often referred to as one of their children—has thrived, educating more than 1,000 students since its opening in September 1972 with 14 students.

My joyous career as an educational leader was only possible because of a dedicated faculty who always put children at the center of their work, whether it was curriculum design, the classroom schedule, or the school calendar. Teachers gave 100 percent, often working in their classrooms in the evenings and weekends. The Board of Trustees was always supportive, providing work, wealth, and wisdom in response to our needs. An active parent community made it possible for faculty and staff to have ambitious visions—yes, the Primary Unit did need your help publishing dozens of the children's "books," the Middle School did recruit you to recite poetry at morning meetings, and we did need you to reheat more than 50 lasagnas for our Thanksgiving Feast.

Without my staff, who oversaw many administrative initiatives and freed me up to be in the classrooms, I could not have been the hands-on educational leader that I wanted to be. Special thanks to my dear friend Nancy Rafferty, who managed the business office expertly, putting up with my sometimes-impossible demands. Fritzi Franks, whom I luckily inherited, served as the school's institutional memory; her work in the areas of development and communications was always faithful to the mission and philosophy of TPS. Abby Levner's grace and caring management of our admissions program introduced hundreds of families to our school and progressive practice; I am grateful for her role as a wise sounding board for many years. Robin Horne, my administrative assistant, "protected" me as she nimbly managed my "open door" office policy. And last but not least, Abbie Siegal-Andrews, our school psychologist. Abbie's empathetic work with teachers, students, and families was brilliant. I thank her for guiding me through some challenging decisions.

As head of school, I benefited from the Board of Trustees and others whose guidance was invaluable. As a new leader of a nonprofit independent school, I was instructed on the nonprofit world by Robert Altman and Jean Mason. Building projects—large and small—were guided by the designs of Philip Franks, Jim Campbell, and Jim Mitchell. How many walls did Phil Franks move to accommodate our changing program and growing student body? Frank Gould's participation in development of the new gymnasium was invaluable. The selfless involvement and financial risks undertaken by Lenny Klehr and Paul Dry enabled the school to purchase what is now the heart of the school's buildings, while the expertise of Dale Levy and Philip Korb shepherded us through the legal complexities involved. In addition, I am grateful for the generosity of the Adelson family, especially for their financial support of the school's outstanding instrumental music programs.

Finally, the children. What a joy it was to watch you learn and grow! And what a joy it was to learn and grow alongside you!

As for this book itself, I am grateful to my editor, Lois West, who improved my writing and challenged my thinking as she did for many years as a member of my administrative team.

Numerous former TPS colleagues have supported this project, clarifying memories and providing archival materials: Anne Greenwald, Barbara Stanley, Marcia Kravis, Abby Levner, Judith Parker, Michael Zimmerman, Dan Lai, and Emily Marston. Special thanks to Janet Weinstein, who read my early chapters and encouraged me to continue. And, thank you, Bill West for proofreading the manuscript.

I would also like to thank Bartley Jeannoute for meeting with me to talk about his research on affinity groups at independent schools. Dr. Vivian Gadsden, the William T. Carter Professor of Child Development and Education at Penn's Graduate School of Education, also generously spoke with me about the developmental appropriateness of affinity groups for middle school students.

Paul Dry encouraged me throughout the writing of this book. It is thanks to Paul Dry Books, here in Philadelphia, that the book is in your hands. Thank you, Paul.

I owe a special debt to friends and family who urged me to continue writing despite the challenges of illness and isolation owing to COVID-19: my sons and daughters and my sister, Nana.

As always, I am grateful to my husband, Mike, for the love and support he has given to me over the years. He edited and proofread drafts of the book, and his accompanying chuckles—"this is great"—kept me going.

Acknowledgments need to be made to Marathon on the Square and the Gran Caffe L'Aquila for allowing me and Lois to linger for hours over lunch in their streeteries as we reviewed chapters during Covid times.

A list of the scores of people who helped me achieve my vision as an educator would go on for pages. I apologize that I could not mention everyone in the text—it truly took a village to accomplish what we did in 23 years.

Printed in the USA
CPSIA information can be obtained
at www.ICGtesting.com
JSHW081907121123
51896JS00001B/21